EILEEN

<u>Nov 95.</u>

To Mum

Belated Happy Birthday

Love
Claire and Gerard

(Billy + Freckles)

EILEEN

Eileen Reid and Jimmy Day

Town House
Dublin

Published in 1995 by
Town House and Country House
Trinity House
Charleston Road
Ranelagh, Dublin 6
Ireland

British Library Cataloguing in Publication Data. A catalogue record for this book is available from the British Library.

ISBN: 1-86059-011-X

Acknowledgements
The authors and publishers would like to thank the following for permission to reproduce photographs: Terence Dunne (nos 6, 7); *Irish Independent* (no 24); Lensmen (no 25); Charlie Collins (no 40); ESB Musical Society (no 41: photo by Alo Brady); Denis O'Ferrall (cover photo and no 42).

The authors extend special thanks to Eileen's mother, to her brother Noel and his wife May, and to her sister Kitty, for their help in sourcing the photos. Thanks are due also to Bob and Marie Fitzpatrick, Síghle Tóibín, Bríd Tunney, Gerry Lundberg, and Sr Theodore of the Holy Faith Convent, Glasnevin, for their help with the photos.

Finally, the authors are indebted to the following: Tommy Moloney, for information on the Liberties, Joe Dodd, for Charlie Reid's football history, Fr Herman Doolan, ODC (Eileen's spiritual director), Fr John McNamara, ODC, and St Theresa's Church, Clarendon Street.

Typeset by Typeform Repro Ltd
Printed in Ireland by Betaprint

For Jimmy

Contents

Illustrations between pages 88 and 105
and between pages 168 and 185

Part One

Liberty girl

I believe there was a bit of a party in our flat shortly after I was born and it's a pity I wasn't old enough to enjoy it. I say this because it was a full twenty years later, on 2 January 1963, before I actually had a birthday party.

The fourth child in a family of seven with four brothers and two sisters, I had seen plenty of sing-songs and hooleys, but alas for yours truly, Eileen Patricia Reid, no birthday party! Having said that, every Sunday dinner was like a birthday celebration in our flat at 18D Block, Iveagh Buildings, Patrick Street, Dublin, because our mother, a professional full-time mammy, saw to it.

The Iveagh Buildings, where I was born, were the brainchild of the first Lord Iveagh, Edward Cecil Guinness. Around 1890 the huge Guinness Brewery was put under the control of a board of directors. This took the pressure off the then proprietor, Edward Cecil, so the kind man turned his mind to reducing the suffering and destitution he saw in the squalled tenements in the old Liberties area of Dublin. He set up the Guinness Trust to help the poor of London and Dublin, but in 1903 the good Lord Iveagh took the funds allotted to Dublin's poor and put them into a separate trust, appropriately called the 'Iveagh Trust', which was set up solely to help the destitute in the old Liberties. To house working-class people in general, he directed the trustees to clear and rebuild on the Bull Alley slums. This resulted in the magnificent red-brick Iveagh Buildings, with their well-designed cheap-rent flats and wonderful recreation areas for children.

Flats were also built at Thomas Court and Kevin Street in the Liberties area, but Lord Iveagh took a shine to the Bull Alley site beside St Patrick's Cathedral, and eventually he used more of his own money on this project than all the funds allotted to London and Dublin. Only the best of materials were used, with the granite blocks and red bricks giving a majestic appearance. The square-shaped plan had four T-shaped five-storey blocks of flats facing each other, with the two opposite sides taken up with a hostel on one and recreation buildings on the other. The space in between contained huge paved playgrounds.

It was like having a safe, cosy, closed-in world of our own. The eight blocks of flats were named in alphabetical order (we lived in D Block), and housed two hundred and fifty families. A typical two-bedroomed flat had a hallway, a bedroom to the side, measuring about 120 square feet, then further on a livingroom which we called the 'middle room', covering about 164 square feet, which separated the first bedroom from the second. A kitchen/scullery off the livingroom had a door leading out onto a small high-railed balcony, which led to a toilet. Later, the balconies were covered in, incorporating the toilet and balcony area into the scullery.

A short southside walk from the Liffey, with Christ Church Cathedral a few hundred yards away on one side and St Patrick's Cathedral nearer still on the other, these Iveagh Buildings were home to the Reid family.

My mother's maiden name was Eileen Thompson. Her father was a native of Belfast and her mother a Dubliner, whereas my dad's father hailed from Blessington, a few miles outside the capital, and his mother from Dublin. As a young couple my mam and dad seemed to be very good with their feet. Miss Thompson, I'm told, could hold her own in any ballroom dancing competition in the country, and Charlie Reid played international soccer for Ireland.

Number 18, a two-bedroomed flat five floors up, at the top, seemed to have ample room for first arrival Noel, followed by Kitty, Charlie Junior, and yours truly, but when Beatrice, Robert and Patrick came along in that order, Number 17, next door, was offered and accepted gratefully. There were four flats to each floor, so as a schoolgirl, when I ran up the sixty-eight concrete steps, without having to touch the heavy black iron balustrade that stretched from the ground floor to our landing at the top, I faced our new flat, Number 17, with 18 beside it to my right. Flat Number 15 was to my left and 16 straight ahead, beside 17.

Heavy bottle-green doors with brass fixtures were the standard entrance to all the flats. The walls of the entire block had white ceramic tiles which ran from the bottom to a border of white tiles with blue flowers half way up, and then painted from there to the ceiling.

Looking out from our back windows, with the playground beneath us, to the south, on our right, was the Iveagh Play Centre, facing Bull Alley. Opposite us to the east were the other four blocks of flats facing onto Bride Street. To our left and north, stood Iveagh Hostel, with its entrance onto Bride Road, and completing the square, westward onto Patrick Street, were the flats in which we lived. Because of its location, Number 17 had no front windows, but the magnificent view from the front of Number 18 more than made up for this. From our high vantage point, with busy Patrick Street below, we could see the Dublin Mountains to our left. We had a panoramic view of the south-west of the city, including all the steeples from the churches in Francis Street, Meath Street and Thomas Street, and even the Wellington Monument in the Phoenix Park.

Below, on the ground floor, there were spaces allotted for small shops, and these were frequented not only by the flat dwellers, but others, including the men from the Iveagh Hostel around the corner. The Iveagh Hostel was for single men and was opened in 1905. The five-storey building had sleeping accommodation for over five hundred men on its upper floors, and the ground floor had all the usual amenities, including reading and smoking rooms and a diningroom. The hostel was spotlessly clean and well run and most of the men we saw coming and going over the years were clean and tidy. There were some, however, who didn't seem to have anywhere else to go, without work or anything to occupy them.

By contrast, life for us was hectic, living in and communicating between two flats, and especially so for the children, sleeping in one and scurrying into the other via the landing for breakfast. I suppose you could call it living in the fast lane, or in our case — landing. All the children slept in Number 18, which had a big double bed in each bedroom, with an extra-large divan bed, which folded up into a leather sofa in the daytime, in the middle room, and a cot thrown in for good measure.

On schooldays we were up at 8 am, and with nothing on except a vest, dashed into Number 17, our feet hardly touching the cold landing floor. We were greeted by a big fire and an even bigger plate of porridge in the livingroom of this one-bedroomed flat where Mam and Dad slept. Mam was awake an hour before us, and as well as having the fire lit and the breakfast cooked, she would have our school clothes at the ready. After washing, I would put on my navy gymslip, white shirt and socks, black shoes and navy jumper, and hope to make it by 9 am to the Holy Faith School, Clarendon Street.

When the last loud goodbye was acknowledged from the landing, Mam would get ready for her daily visit to the Iveagh markets nearby. Having no fridge in those days, the food was bought fresh every day. The way Mam fed us you'd think we were all entered in a 'heaviest child in the buildings' competition. She bought rashers, sausages, pigs' feet, ham, black and white puddings and salted ribs in such quantities that I thought the pig might become an endangered species. If we were Jewish instead of Catholic, I think we might have starved to death. She bought other meats as well and did a great job in varying the dinners each day. We had a big Irish stew once a week and a Dublin coddle of ham pieces, rashers and sausages and potatoes every Saturday. Salted ribs with cabbage and big 'flowery' potatoes were among my favourites. With lambs' liver and hearts and fresh vegetables every day, she was one of Clarkes Butchers' best customers.

A trip to the Iveagh fish market was a must every Friday, and the way Mam cooked seafood was a joy to watch. Whole fish deep-fried with flour in a batter or cooked in a pan was delicious. Mam was an artist with fish and would give the famous Burdock's fish and chip shop near Christ Church a run for their money when it came to preparing battered cod or whiting. My dad used to throw the heads and tails of the fish out through the back window onto a nearby roof and the seagulls would catch some of them in mid-air and swallow them whole. The gulls came around every Friday, like clockwork, at the same time, and created a fierce noise outside the back window.

Fish heads weren't the only thing thrown out the window. If we got hungry while playing in the yard below, we'd shout, or rather scream, up to our mother to put some jam sandwiches or biscuits in a bag and throw them down to us. Any cricket team in the world would have been proud of the catches we made. Mam also used to put some oatmeal on the two-foot-wide window sill of Number 17 for the pigeons, and they would literally knock on the window with their beaks if she forgot.

'Unforgettable' would be the word to describe the smell of the fresh bread and cakes coming from Kennedy's bakery in Patrick Street. On weekdays, women coming back from ten o'clock Mass couldn't resist slipping in for their fresh cream slices, and the temptation of picking a hole in the hot 'turnover' I was sent to buy, resulted in me having to volunteer to take the 'slice with the hole' when the bread was cut for the tea.

We seemed to get better value for money in those days. Even a Swiss roll was half a size bigger than it would be now, and packaged food seemed to have bigger boxes. We got the best value of all every Friday when Mrs Conroy, who lived two floors below us in Number 7, gave us three tickets to exchange for broken biscuits in Jacob's. When I was given the tickets I'd go to the back of Jacob's factory in Bishop Street, a few minutes' walk away, between five and six o'clock in the evening, and a man would give me one large bag of broken biscuits, a second bag containing marshmallows, and the third bag had chocolate biscuits, and on rare occasions we were treated to a bag of chocolate sweets.

Mrs Conroy's daughter May married my brother Noel many years later and they are still very happy, living in Rathfarnham with grown-up children. I hasten to add that broken biscuits, via Mrs Conroy's tickets, weren't the only ones we ate. In Butler's shop beneath our flat we used to get things like the newspaper, packets of biscuits, cheese and milk, and put them on 'the slate', meaning we didn't have to pay until the end of the week. I remember how awkward it was if Butler's didn't have some item and I'd have to go to a shop further along, that served C Block. If I walked in first and a couple of C Block regulars came in behind me, they would be served first. I think I wouldn't have been served at all if greed didn't overcome resentment.

Saturday was a very busy day for us because most of it was spent preparing for our best day — Sunday. My older sister, Kitty, was a great worker at home, a sort of second mammy, and did most of the cleaning and polishing on Saturday before I was old enough to help. When that time came, Mam used to give me sixpence to clean and polish Number 18. The sixpence was left on the sideboard and I never touched it until I was finished the work. I would even lift it up to polish underneath and then leave it back. The polish came from tins and the shine from dry cloths and muscle power. The halldoors' knobs, knockers and numbers were shined up with Brasso, as was the tea-set on the sideboard with the 'belly-front' and sixpence on top in the middle room. All the linen, including tablecloths, bed sheets and blankets, and some lace curtains and heavier outer ones, were kept in the sideboard. When the floors were washed and polished and everything done, it was dinner time and we could sit down and 'polish off' the coddle which was simmering for hours on the stove.

Not everyone was happy with the shiny floors. The boys used to complain that, in your stocking feet, you could slip and 'break your snot' if you weren't careful. This didn't bother me as I collected my sixpence and thought of the variety of sweets I could buy with all this money. Caramels were twelve for a penny and two big toffees were the same price, and then there was a 'sailor's chew' — decisions, decisions.

The siesta Mam took in the afternoon was both necessary and deserved. Lying down for an hour gave her back the energy for what lay ahead. After her rest, every Saturday, when we were very young, immediately after our tea, it was bath time. We didn't have a fixed bath in those days so she washed us in a big grey enamel bath in front of a roaring fire in the middle room. She'd put towels on the table, wash us with a big bar of Lifebuoy soap, sit us on the table and dry us.

This same enamel bath, with the help of a scrubbing board, was used to do the washing on Mondays in Number 17. The old reliable red or white carbolic soap wasn't spared. As soon as the clothes were washed, they were rinsed, with the tap running, in the sink. A mangle was used to squeeze the heavy wet from the now clean clothes. For stubborn areas like collars and cuffs of shirts, a small brush was used to get the dirt off. I remember how Mam's knuckles were swollen from constant rubbing against the scrubbing board. It was difficult to dry clothes then, but she always managed, despite making the flat look like an explosion in a laundry. There were clothes anywhere there was heat, including the scullery, clothes horses and fireguards.

In contrast, although Saturday was busy, the hard labour was missing. With our shoes polished and clothes ironed, the last thing she did before going for a social drink with friends was to prepare the meats, greens and potatoes. Pots of food covered with water were left on the gas stove with nothing to do except 'put a light' under them on Sunday morning.

Larry and Maureen Rowantree and Mr and Mrs John Brocklebank were probably Mam's most constant companions in Cunnynham's lounge in Lord Edward Street for a Saturday night 'chinwag'. My dad very very rarely joined my mam at this social gathering.

Having gone to Confession on Saturday, we would regularly receive Communion at nine o'clock Mass in St Nicholas of Myra's church, and the only thing on our minds running home afterwards was the big fry-up which was traditional on Sunday mornings. Fried bread was popular then, as well as the usual eggs, sausages, rashers and black and white pudding. In very cold weather the table was placed near the fire so that we could thaw out and fill up at the same time. After Sunday breakfast, if any of us went to play with pals, we were always told to stay within the boundaries of the flats and not to talk to strangers. In fact, we never played anywhere else because we had all we needed in the confines of the Iveagh Buildings. After playing, a little more carefully in our Sunday clothes, the energy we spent was more than replaced by a dinner fit for any celebration. Roast beef and lamb, vegetables of all kinds, potatoes mashed or roasted, five big apple cakes and a large pot of custard were consumed and then washed down with milk, tea or lemonade. Some cabbage water was kept because it was highly recommended for purifying the blood, toning the skin and in some cases turning the stomach. Before Mam would take a nap but not before she dipped into her purse, some of us were off to the Tivoli or Green Picture House.

The Tivoli cinema in Francis Street was nicknamed 'the flea house', at least the fourpenny part of it was. Flash Gordon was a favourite of mine because each episode would finish up with 'Flash', a space hero, about to be squashed or hanging on to life by his finger tips. I just couldn't wait until the following Sunday to see what happened next. We used to call these short films 'follyin uppers'. Flash Gordon would fly around in something that looked like a washing machine compared to today's 'Star Wars' epics, but we enjoyed it just the same. Although these Sunday afternoon picture shows were a treat we looked forward to, I always remember how really happy I was on my way home, knowing that Mam was always there, and how disappointed I was, on the rare occasion, when I arrived to find she had gone out.

This was typical family life, as it was, and as I loved it, in the heart of the Liberties, and in the unique atmosphere of the Iveagh Buildings.

School — the 'Bayno' of my life

Academically speaking, I think it would have been better if my long-suffering teachers had left me playing with the *marla* or putty they first gave me when I arrived, aged four, at St Bridget's Holy Faith School, Clarendon Street. With these six-inch strips, I was as happy as a pig in sunshine making little men with little arms, legs, heads and bellies. Unfortunately, things were going to get a little more complicated than this.

I hated going to school on cold mornings, and one of the reasons for this was the warm milk that was supplied with a sandwich during a break after our 9 am start. The milk was cold coming in by truck through the big gates at the back entrance in Balfe Street, but then the half-pint bottles were put on the hot pipes in the classroom to take the chill out of them. I didn't drink the milk but I did eat the jam sandwich that came with it. On alternative days I would take the cheese sandwich or the corned beef, but the milk remained the same, hot and untouched. Isn't it strange how little things like this stick in one's mind.

Sr Liguori was the principal of the school, but we also had lay teachers. Some of the tutors' names that come to mind are Miss McDermott, Miss Connolly who taught us dancing, Mr Goddard our gym instructor, Sister Dolorosa in Communion class, and Sister Lorcan in Confirmation class.

As I settled in and reached the stage where I was able to walk home at midday unaccompanied by my mother, I could easily do the return trip between 12.45 pm and 1.30 pm. The afternoons were quite short compared to the mornings, and when the final school bell rang at 3.15 pm, the real fun began. The doors were opened, the children were running, the direction was home, the object was play, and I was no exception.

I probably had the best crèche and playground Dublin has ever seen, the Iveagh Play Centre. The Bayno, as it was affectionately known, was part of the Iveagh Buildings and had marvellous facilities. The play centre was opened in 1915, funded entirely by Lord Iveagh, and was architecturally far superior to the rest of the buildings. It was originally located at Myra Hall in Francis Street, where, on 8 July 1911, King George V and his wife Queen Mary made a royal visit.

I think the Bayno got its name from the word Beano, which was Dublin 'slang' for feast. Dublin children, including myself, had the habit of never using a full word when half of it would do. The Beano, or feast, was the bun and cocoa supplied free between 4 pm and 6 pm every weekday in the recreation hall at the centre. I remember how, at 4 pm each day, after school, with boys in one line and girls in another, we marched into the big hall to the sound of a piano and all singing 'Good Evening to You'. The girls would curtsy and the boys would salute to a very important-looking lady standing on a podium. The lady would welcome us and express the wish that we would enjoy ourselves. Women in white aprons would fill up enamel mugs with 'Shell' cocoa, and then wicker baskets full of fresh currant buns were handed out.

The ladies who ran the Bayno spoke 'ever-so-grand' and they taught us to sew and cook and dance, with everything supplied free of charge. We even had a library at our disposal. It was essential to be orderly and mannerly and anyone causing trouble would be asked to leave and never let back into the centre. The big Bayno yard was well used in the summertime. Sometimes a piano was brought out and while a lady played we danced around the Maypole. We organised our own sports and games, and enjoyed the thrills of the egg-and-spoon race, the three-legged race and the sack race. Releav-y-o, hop scotch, piggy bed and hoops were common games, and when for a while roller skating was all the go, everyone had to get a pair, until some other fad came along.

Running and gymnastics were right up my street. Being double-jointed, I could walk like a crab with my head between my legs, do the splits and cartwheels, and use my inherited leg muscles to run the pins off most of the kids in the Bayno yard. Being fast had its advantages when playing 'Catch a Girl, Kiss a Girl', because I could use my speed to get away from this guy with specs who insisted on chasing me all the time. When I asked him why he didn't chase someone else for a change, he told me it was because he liked me. I then got a brainwave and invented a game called 'Catch a Boy, Kiss a Boy', so I could run down the boy I fancied, avoiding you know who like the plague.

The playground was a very safe place for children to play, protected with big iron gates which were closed at certain times, and mothers could actually shout out through open windows when their offsprings' grub was ready. We wouldn't go to the Bayno every day, but coming up to Christmas we would make sure to go on a regular basis because we wanted to be in the concert and be certain of our Christmas present. Regulars were picked for parts in a concert that was directed by the ladies in charge, and the experience was great fun as well as being educational. There was a party afterwards and everyone got a present.

These were happy days for me, despite the fact that the sum total of my academic ability was failure in the Primary Certificate, and I was encouraged along life's journey by being told by my head teacher that I would go nowhere. Yet I regret nothing of my childhood and wouldn't, if I could, change a thing. The Iveagh flats and play centre gave me the opportunities to read and write and sing and dance and swim and play with the same happy, carefree, indestructible attitude I inherited from my mother.

Some 7.8 million children passed through the Iveagh Play

Centre from its opening in 1915 until it closed in 1975. If the Bayno was around today, membership would be difficult to obtain and it would be only for the élite. I would have loved my children to have had such an experience.

Battle of conscience

I kept no secrets from Mam, I told her everything, and did everything she asked me to do. This was one of the reasons, I suppose, why my younger sister, Beatrice, never played with me. Beatrice called me 'Gawky Order' and made sure I wasn't around when she was doing something she didn't want my mother to know about. I never knew what 'Gawky Order' meant but I knew it was closely linked with 'Stupid'. I may not have been as streetwise as Beatrice but I was never easily led and certainly not stupid enough to fall into the duck pond in St Stephen's Green. Beatrice managed this feat when a gang of us armed with six-foot pinkeen rods visited the Green, which is about fifteen minutes' walk from the flats. The rods had nets on top of them and we would simply reach into the pond and catch pinkeens to put in jam jars.

A pinkeen as large as the 'one that got away' was spotted by Beatrice, whose enthusiasm to catch it belly-flopped her into the water. We fished her out and, under the shade of the nearest tree, we formed a circle and discreetly stripped her, knickers and all. She borrowed a slip and cardigan and we marched her home, surrounding her like Nero's guard.

Maureen Malone was my best friend. She was tall and pretty with shiny curly brown hair. The curls, or ringlets, were about two inches thick, the same length all around, and when she walked they bounced up and down like jelly. I never had ringlets, my hair being cut in a 'bob', straight, chin-length, blonde, split to the left and caught with a bow or slide, over to the right. Some mothers had great success creating ringlets in their little girls' hairs with the use of rags or pipe cleaners. I tried this once and the next morning I had a head of wool. I looked like I was plugged into a light socket.

Maureen lived in A Block and we were great pals, visiting each other's flats, confiding in each other and playing together after school. Of course, even living in the comparative safety of the buildings is not the perfect world and mothers were not the only ones watching little girls playing. Part of the game of releav-y-o involved getting a twenty-second headstart to hide yourself somewhere before one of your friends, who was supposed to have her eyes closed, came looking for you. I was hiding on the landing of a nearby flat when a young lad I knew well, came along and offered me sweets from a big brown bag. He started to explain the facts of life to me, but at five years old I was more interested in the sweets than what he produced when he then exposed himself. He said he wouldn't harm me and told me not to be afraid. At his next suggestion I forgot about my sweet tooth, said no, laughed, then ran off to tell my friends who were finishing the game of releav-y-o to hurry, there were sweets on offer on the landing. They just shrugged off what I said, telling me that he was always doing that and to stay away from him.

To this day I can't understand the young fellow's audacity. Anyone could have opened the door and caught him. Nevertheless, at five years old I somehow instinctively knew that what the guy with the sweets was doing was wrong. As for myself, I was never taught the facts of life, either at home or at school. I remember a group of us were standing in the Bayno yard and a friend, Bridie Rodgers, came up to us and told us that she had found out that babies came from women's bums. We all broke our hearts laughing, saying that this was a physical impossibility. I was laughing because I already knew that babies came from heads of cabbage — my mother had told me! Would you believe that this incident took place when I was, wait for it, twelve years old?

I was just about out of the land of nod with regards to

where babies came from when something else happened, which I knew nothing about, and this nearly cost me my sanity. I was thirteen, and a group of us, all girls, went out, by bus, to Seapoint. It was a lovely summer's day and with only a bathing suit, towel and a few bob to spend, we were looking forward to enjoying ourselves on this popular beach between Blackrock and Dún Laoghaire. As soon as we arrived, it was a case of 'Last one into the water buys the drinks', as everyone awkwardly wrestled into bathing suits, modesty guarded only by a towel. I wasn't minding what anyone in particular was saying amid the excited chatter, but when Maura Duffy said 'there's a blood stain on the back of your dress', I had her undivided attention. As my pals scampered down to the water, my eyes confirmed but couldn't believe what they saw. When? Why? How did this happen? What was going to happen next and what could I do about it? I had to get home fast. I put my bathing suit on and my dress on over it, and rolled my pants up in a towel. Then, with the towel in one hand and my other hand holding on, like a drowning man's grip, to that part of my dress with the offending stain, I headed for the bus.

There were only two people on the bus besides me, yet I stood all the way home. I was invited to sit by the conductor and again by one of the two passengers, but I politely refused. How could they know I was holding on to the greatest mystery since the so-called big bang. I don't think Moses was as relieved to see the sea parting as I was to see my mam talking to a neighbour on the top landing of D Block. I had made it, help was at hand, Mam would surely solve everything. I didn't know whether to laugh or cry when the answer to my whisper in her ear was 'Is that all? I'll be in in a minute, you'll be all right'. So much for sex education in the fifties.

Mam was a genius at saying a lot and telling you nothing, as she was also a genius at supplying plenty from seemingly nothing. She always seemed to be robbing Peter to pay Paul, and then giving back to Peter again, until it got to the stage that no one knew who had the money, Peter, Paul, or my mother. She used to get 'dockets' to a certain value and trade them for goods, mostly clothes, in places like Cassidys, and then over a period of time pay back to the person who had supplied the dockets their monetary value.

This system was very handy for Communion and Confirmation clothes, at Christmastime, and for other such financial emergencies. Everything was done on trust, with no legal documents involved. Weekly payments of some kind or another were a constant ritual at home. Beatrice and I used to get the same style dress, bought in Cassidys, in different colours, perhaps a pink one for me and blue for Beatrice. When we got older, say about fifteen, Mam went to a Mrs Keating who sold lovely designer dresses fit for young ladies.

A young lady I certainly was not, judging by the confrontations I had over the years with my tutors and my conscience. A very dark but good example of this comes to mind. At home we were all brought up to be strictly honest, but my love for things that sparkled led me to do something that I thought I would never do and would rather forget. I was eight years old at the time and I saw a necklace, Woolworth's finest, that I fell madly in love with. The necklace belonged to the older sister of Concepta Gleeson. Concepta, who was in my class in school, brought the necklace with her and was showing it off to the other girls in the classroom. She kept it in an Anadin box, and when we all jumped up to go to lunch, the box fell on the floor. She didn't pick it up, so without hesitation I stooped down and put it in my pocket.

I'm ashamed to say I kept it and even had the cheek to wear it openly in the Bayno yard. Concepta saw me wearing the necklace but said nothing. Afterwards I gave it to my older sister, Kitty, who wore it to a dance at which Concepta's sister, the real owner, was present. Kitty, of course, didn't know the sinister history of the necklace and danced away in innocent ignorance. That battle with my conscience was lost, but I'm glad to say, from then on, things that sparkled were admired but never touched.

Speaking of battles, the Battle of Clontarf is significant for me for two reasons. One! it was the only history question I knew the answer to, and two! I felt I was in it when it came to doing sums. '1014' I'd pipe up when the date of the battle was asked, and then I would pipe down for the rest of the class. History for me was one long boring episode of English wars and Irish uprisings and never figured in any of my daydreams. Arithmetic was even worse. Being slapped for every sum I got wrong made me think that maybe I should take the slaps instead of the sums before I went home and save everyone a lot of time and trouble. I got so desperate on one occasion that I got my older brother Noel to do my sums for me. This turned out to be a disaster because I was the only one in the class to get the hardest sum right. My 'bewildered' teacher couldn't wait to bring me up to the top of the class to explain this mathematical mystery to the lesser mortals in front of me. With chalk in my hand and nothing in my head I stood at the blackboard wondering what the odds were against an earthquake hitting the school. Instead, the teacher's hand hit my face and the little wire glasses I wore for reading flew across the room. The whole sorry tale ended with titters from my classmates, a tongue-lashing from my teacher, tears from my eyes and a disgusting flow from my nose that stuck to everything it touched.

In case you think I was a complete idiot, I would like to say that I could make a success out of anything I really put my mind to. I felt I was geared more to physical things, and this observation was seconded by my drill instructor, Mr Goddard. He was tall, dark, slim and handsome and looked immaculate in his white shirt, cream slacks and sweater, and white runners. Our teacher, Miss McDermott, was pretty and petite, and I got the impression she had a soft eye for him. When he wanted to demonstrate a particular drill, he would always bring me up onto the platform. Standing behind me he would hold my arms out straight, and when pushing them forward, brought a big 'oooh' from the infatuated girls as his arms came around me. He got a great laugh out of this, but I always thought Miss McDermott was not amused. During our practice sessions he would shout 'Watch Eileen' as I coasted through an intricate display of kicks and steps from the front of the drill team. We got to the final of an inter-schools drill display competition, and on that fateful day we lost because, according to our school heads, there was no Eileen to watch.

No, I wasn't sick, I was in Howth with Mam, Beatrice and two of my brothers, Robert and Patrick. I thought I wouldn't be missed, surely there were enough of them to carry on. No one would speak to me when I got to school the next day. Sr Liguori said I was selfish and a disgrace to the school and I would never be included in any recreation projects again.

'Talented but giddy' would be the apt phrase to describe my contribution to the church choir. I not only enjoyed singing in the choir but I also enjoyed being in the church. I felt happy there and always got involved in any of the religious ceremonies taking place. Being in the choir meant singing at High Mass on Sunday, all the sodalities and retreats, Christmas and Easter celebrations, miraculous medal devotion on Monday nights, and any other church activity that required the gift of music. I could view the church from the window of Number 18. I remember looking out one night and seeing the lights on, and rushing around to find out what I was missing. When I got there I was told that the church was being cleaned.

Making my first Holy Communion was a big thrill and I can recall going to Confession for the first time. For my sins I did a lot of soul searching and finally settled for 'I cursed, told lies and was disobedient'. We never had any Bible classes but I understood the main things about God and the Trinity and the Apostles. I used to talk to God a lot and ask him for things like one more hour of sunshine so we could stay outside and play. I knew God was 'magic' and didn't need anything, so I was always asking, thinking that I could give him nothing. I had a great view of the clouds from my window and, particularly when I was sick and had plenty of time to spare, I'd watch the birds 'going home' in the evening and have little one-sided conversations with God. I remember very clearly, when the scenes of the canonisation of Saint Pope Pius X were being broadcast on the radio and when the broadcaster declared that the new saint's soul was now about to enter Heaven, rushing to the window and looking at the sky. The whole sky was covered with thick black clouds with not a break in sight. Suddenly I saw a gold-coloured light penetrating the clouds, shining very brightly, and then fading. I shouted to my mother to come and see the saint going to Heaven, but she just laughed and dismissed it. I didn't mind that, but being dismissed from the church choir was a little harder to take.

'Choir means a group of singers sounding like one' was a piece of information definitely meant for me, as the choir mistress glared into my face. What she really meant was that during practice, the choir was heard all over the church, but Eileen Reid was heard all over the Liberties. The trouble with this was, when I got a fit of the giggles, my voice was missed from the ensemble. This happened once too often, and hence the dismissal.

I still loved singing and valued my vocal chords far too much to indulge in a new adventure called 'smoking'. 'Where does the smoke go?' I asked as fifteen of us broke up five woodbines and set fire to the pieces in the Bayno yard. When I saw some of my pals going blue in the face from coughing and others pulling pieces of tobacco, with skin still attached, from their lips, I said 'Who needs this?' and a life-long goodbye to that habit. My mates took a dim view of me not taking 'a drag'. Kids are a bit cruel when one of their own doesn't row-in with what is generally accepted. I suppose I became a victim of the 'She never does anything' syndrome — the 'anything' to me was something I would rather think about before doing.

Abnormalities are, when noticed by adults, discreetly commented on, but children, bless their honest, open hearts, have far less inhibitions in this regard. 'Hey, dyed head!' was a hurtful comment that had me anxiously asking my mother 'Why are they jeering me?'. What my mother didn't tell me, as my baby blonde hair got a little darker with age, was that she was putting peroxide in my hair to make me a more 'natural' blonde. What she did tell me was 'Don't mind them, they are only jealous'.

Having dyed hair was a blessing compared with being a diphtheria carrier. Being all alone in an isolation ward in hospital, aged seven, wasn't very pleasant. My whole day was spent looking out of a window and I felt like royalty waving from a balcony on visiting day. One day Mam and Dad were called in and asked for their permission for a new drug to be used on me. The drug was called Penicillin. They consented and it worked. Today I am allergic to it. One tiny dose and I turn into the Elephant Man, or rather, Woman.

As if that wasn't enough, I then wound up in a convalescent home recovering from rheumatic fever. I can remember walking around an orchard there, collecting apples in a basket. What was weird and unforgettable was being washed in the same bath water as a dozen other kids. When it came to my turn the water was filthy. I was washed, half dried, including my hair, dressed and sent out to play. When I returned to health I was certainly glad to be out of that place.

Hands, knees and Auntie Beattie

A memorable and happy part of my childhood was spent in the company of my Auntie Beattie. Auntie Beattie was one of my mother's three sisters and she lived in F Block of the Iveagh Buildings, which faced out onto Bride Street. Mam's second sister, Annie, lived on the same landing as ourselves, in flat 15, while the third sister had emigrated to England. Auntie Beattie's second-floor one-bedroomed flat was tastefully furnished and immaculately kept. She herself was tall, blonde, glamorous and ladylike, with poise and elegance that would be the envy of any model. Her husband was Peadar Gaskins who played international soccer for Ireland alongside my own father.

I used to visit them occasionally and remember how kind they were to me, particularly one Christmas when they told me that Santy had left something in their flat and presented me with my first doll's house, complete with furniture inside. Tragedy struck the couple, who lost their three children, one stillborn and the other two living just a few months. Auntie Beattie suffered from a kidney ailment which affected the infants. When Peadar was forty-two years old he caught pneumonia and died, leaving her alone and devastated. After her very well-known husband's huge funeral, Auntie Beattie, who loved him dearly, went into deep mourning. I was six years old at the time and to keep her company I used to visit her after school. She wore black clothes for three years, until finally she gave in to pressure from family and friends to get on with her life.

Auntie Beattie became a great friend and soon my visits extended to overnight stays. These became so frequent that

I saw very little of my own home. Mam didn't like this idea and, having sent for me, explained her anxiety. Twice a week visits were now in order and I looked forward to these enjoyable novelties.

My favourite auntie was gifted with the craft of sewing and this was evident by her beautiful embroidery work. Red flowers and green leaves adorned tablecloths, and cushions displayed her personal sewing touch. To earn some extra money she would make rag dolls, and I used to help her put them in bundles of twelve, ready for the factory, where the plastic face would be attached.

Auntie Beattie had expensive clothes and jewellery, crocodile shoes and hats of all styles in their own boxes. 'Don't finger the hat' she'd tell me as I'd try one on, decked out in some of her jewellery and clip-clopping around the flat in high-heeled shoes three sizes too big for me. She bought me lovely little dresses so I could wear them on the occasions when she'd bring me down town to see the lights and to window shop. We'd walk over O'Connell Bridge and down Henry Street and enjoy looking at the clothes and hats and shoes in the big department stores. I got very possessive of my auntie and if she ever mentioned remarrying I'd get very unhappy. She used to tease me a little about this and one time she introduced me to her insurance agent as the new man in her life. She asked me if I liked him and I said no, and I told him to his face that he couldn't come into Auntie Beattie's flat. I said it wasn't his house and if they married I'd never come to visit her again.

Even though Auntie Beattie smoked herself, she warned me about smoking. She showed me the filter she used in her cigarette holder. The little sugary-looking particles turned brown as the smoke passed through and she explained that my lungs would look like that if I smoked.

She even tried to improve my diction, bravely battling to turn my dese and dose into these and those. She told me never to curse, which my mam also told me. She told me to have good manners, which my mam also told me. She also told me that my name was Irene, not Eileen, which my mam reversed and told me to keep it that way.

A radiogram was a rare thing to see in the flats and I made full use of the one Auntie Beattie had. Her record collection was very limited but of high quality. She wouldn't mind repeatedly putting on the big 78 rpm discs and listening to me singing along to Strauss waltzes, the melodies of which I got to know off by heart. The top notes of Gracie Fields and Joan Sutherland became no problem to my developing voice range. Inevitably, tunes like 'I'm in Love with Vienna' and 'Oh My Beloved Father' gave way a few years later to a couple of popular songs by an artist who would have an influence on me in the future. Auntie Beattie never bought pop records but she made an exception when she treated me to a helping of Connie Francis.

It was not long after this that my beloved auntie died. I was fourteen years old when I heard the news that Auntie Beattie had collapsed and died outside Siney's shop in Golden Lane, a few hundred yards from her flat. It was 2 December and she was carrying some Christmas shopping. A blood clot to the brain was the cause of death and this I believe was in consequence of an old foot injury she received many years previously. She was to be married to the new man in her life the following April. I'll never forget my Auntie Beattie and I'll always pray for her.

While my vocal chords got exercised in places like Auntie Beattie's flat, the rest of my body was bursting with frustrated energy. I was bored hanging around the flats and wanted to use the tremendous vitality that I had. Never liking to 'run with the herd', I knew that there was more to life than what I was doing. I had to push myself forward to more exciting things because I knew nobody else would. I began to 'sniff out' what was going on outside my Iveagh Buildings' environment, and one day my curiosity brought me inside the Green Lounge Restaurant on St Stephen's Green. I was eight at the time and was probably on my way home from a trip to St Stephen's Green when I heard the sound of music and dancing coming from the restaurant. Unafraid, I walked in, and after enquiring, I was told that there were dancing lessons in progress in a room at the back of the restaurant. I was allowed to go in, and during a break in the lesson a lady enquired if she could help me. I asked if it would be all right if I watched, she said it would, and I stood there until the end of the lesson. The children were doing mostly ballet and a little tap dancing. 'Can you dance?' the lady asked in answer to my desire to join the class. I danced a little routine with the children, then she brought me over to the ballet bar and lifted my leg up. She was obviously amazed that my leg went straight up above my head. I then did the splits on her request and she said she would be delighted to have me in the class.

Over the next few weeks I got on very well with this extremely kind and respectable lady. One day she told me that the dancing troop was going to England for two weeks and she wanted to take me along. When I broke the news at home my mam said, 'Why do you join these things? These people have money. You'll need ballet shoes and leotards and all sorts of things. You'd be better off out of there.' I had noticed that the mothers and children associated with the class were very upper class. The mothers had bags and mufflers and matching hats, coats and shoes, and the children had all the gear, leotards, tutus and ballet shoes. I didn't care if I danced in my bathing costume as long as I was part of it all.

Mam said no to the trip. I cried and said I wouldn't need much equipment, trying to make it sound inexpensive. I then suggested wearing my Sunday dress to the lessons in case she stopped me from going altogether. Then the lady instructor asked to meet my mam to discuss ways of overcoming any problems, but the meeting never took place. I couldn't understand Mam's way of thinking and was confused and shed more tears when my teacher said it was no use continuing to dance if I could go nowhere. It was a terrible waste, she said.

From there, I journeyed over to another dancing class in Warrenmount School, off the Coombe in the Liberties. Some of my friends, including Patty Little and Maura Duffy, were already attending the class. It was here I met an experienced gymnastics teacher who took a shine to me. She asked me if she could train me, saying that my body was so supple I was half way towards making a fine gymnast already. I was delighted and said yes, but it involved expense and my mother said no.

I was hurt and frustrated and began to think that any ambitious dreams I had would remain dreams. But then maybe I was selfish, after all, Mam did know best. I loved her very much and appreciated the constant hard work she put into providing each of us with all the attention and comforts she could possibly give us. She was all in favour of me dancing and singing and doing gymnastics, but money was needed for more important things. I felt hard done by, but then, I didn't have to feed and clothe and school seven children.

Don't put your daughter . . .

When a person gets to the stage where they feel they have to advance or stagnate, decisions must be made. I was doing the same things dancewise for a couple more years when I felt I had to learn more. I heard that relations of Mrs Murphy, who lived nearby in John Dillon Street, ran a dancing school, so I decided to enquire. 'Yes,' said Mrs Murphy, when she opened the door to me, 'it's Nora and Margaret Flanagan you're after, they run a school in Parnell Square.'

I joined the class and began to learn some fancy footwork. Some of the Theatre Royal's famous Royalettes were taught here by the Flanagan sisters and some of them later formed their own classes. The Flanagan school of dancing had a higher standard of discipline and technique than I had known previously and I settled in very well. A few months later our school's 'Queen of Taps' competition was one of the attractions at the annual variety show in the hall in Parnell Square. Mam, looking very glamorous, was as proud as punch watching her ten-year-old daughter taking second place. When I walked up to the lord mayor to collect my medal, dressed in a red majorette jacket, gold buttons and a very short white skirt, showing everything it was supposed to cover, he told me that I would definitely win the following year. When the Flanagan sisters added my acrobatic ability to the tap steps, they were impressed, and teamed me up with another young dancer to work out a routine. This other dancer was Billy Boyle, who later made a big name for himself in the entertainment business in England. The routine we were taught involved doing the splits, cartwheels and synchronised tap-dancing. It was perfected to such a degree that Billy and I were offered a spot on a variety show in the Theatre Royal for a week.

We were both thrilled with the offer and I ran home excitedly to tell my mother. She brought me crashing down to earth again with one word — no! 'Your father doesn't want you up on a stage,' she said, hinting that they both believed the entertainment business had a sinister aura about it. Dancing in little white skirts in front of mammies and daddies at the local hall was one thing, but kicking your legs up in front of paying customers in a theatre was quite another matter.

Billy did the spot on his own and his career took off. The Flanagan sisters didn't know what to do with me then, because they couldn't put me in with the older girls of seventeen and eighteen, and so they brought me as far as I could go at my age. I thought at this stage that I probably would have to wait till I was twenty-one before I could strut my stuff anywhere really public, and in the meantime I would be 'dancing with tears in my eyes'.

Luckily the Iveagh Baths were literally around the corner from me on Bride Road, where I could indulge more frequently now in my other passion — swimming. In a couple of years I was beginning to compete with the best, getting my experience with the Guinness swimming club and winning medals in the breaststroke, my forte in the water. Julia Coyne was among many very nice people I met at the baths. She was a fine swimmer and offered to coach me, thinking there was a future for me in swimming. Although I got a life-saving certificate at thirteen and loved swimming, it was not to figure greatly in my future. I really enjoyed attending the galas held in the baths, which attracted a very 'jolly hockey stick', well-to-do crowd, and an occasional visit by my dad who approved wholeheartedly of my interest in swimming.

The lure of the stage was still very strong, so when I spotted an advertisement in the paper for entry to a talent competition I thought, here's my chance to sing in front of people and it won't cost anything. Following instructions, I found myself standing in a queue on a long stairway of a big house somewhere on Fitzwilliam Square. It must have been a big competition because there seemed to be hundreds there. The queue went right down the street. I thought at the time that the hopefuls around me all came from Fitzwilliam Square, judging by their posh accents. They were ever so 'law-di-daw' and every single person had a case of some kind or other with them. There were fiddle cases, cello and viola cases and even briefcases, with me probably the only hard case among them. I had neither music nor instrument, just a young girl standing in a dress and cardigan looking up at these adult, well-organised, intelligent, highly talented-looking people. I was getting some peculiar looks, but nobody was unmannerly enough to ask me, if I wasn't wasting my time, what was I doing there. As I got nearer to the audition room I was bombarded with all sorts of sounds, screeching fiddles, wailing cellos, roaring tenors and warbling sopranos. There are no pop singers here at all, I thought, but I held my ground.

My entrance into the room was like walking in on a court martial with the death sentence already announced. There was an awful foreboding in the air. There were two men and three women sitting at a table and they all looked bored out of their brains. A tall man, about seventy years old, was standing beside a piano. He had grey hair and was dressed in a light grey suit and he didn't look too pleased either. The last person in the room, a young man, took my name and address, and then it was showtime.

'What are you going to sing, Miss Reid?' I was asked.

'Stupid Cupid,' I said.

'Stupid Cupid, what is that? Have you any music?'

'No,' I said.

It was then that the old man in the grey suit, who was the piano player, came into the picture. He approached me as if

I was contagious and said, 'I've never heard of this song. What key do you sing it in?'

'I don't know anything about keys — just follow me,' I said.

'We don't do that sort of thing, you have to have music.'

'All right then,' I said, 'I'll sing it on my own.'

The piano player was highly annoyed, I could read his thoughts — 'this little upstart dispensing with my services.'

The man who took my name announced to the panel of judges that I was Eileen Reid of 18D Iveagh Buildings, Patrick Street, and I was going to sing 'Stupid Cupid'. Then they started, 'Stupid Cupid, what's that?' I told them it was on the back of a Connie Francis record. This useless piece of information didn't help matters so, in order not to cause any more embarrassment, they told me to carry on. I walked up to the microphone, situated beside the piano, and belted out 'Stupid Cupid, you're a real mean guy'. That's as far as I got. They all jumped up together like performing dolphins, their hands up as if their hearing aids had exploded. Hold on Miss Reid, you've got a very strong voice, maybe you should move back from the microphone. I moved about three yards away to the middle of the room and without any microphone used my hands and body movements to put the song across with such energy that even this panel of undertakers started smiling and clapping along to the beat. When I had finished they clapped and told me that they really enjoyed it, I was a breath of fresh air, and they would be in touch with me.

As I walked back home I thought that was the end of it, I would hear nothing more. However, shortly afterwards I received a letter saying that I had been selected to progress in the competition. I hoped it wasn't me who put the kiss of death on it because I heard later that the whole thing was called off.

Whiskey on a Sunday

I'm sorry to say that although he lived until he was eighty-two, I never really knew my dad. My relationship with him turned out to be one long sad but important lesson in life. To say he was fond of the drink would be an understatement because he was either drunk or working on it most of his married life.

It all seemed to go wrong when his soccer career ended. He was always in control during the heady days when his name was constantly in the sports pages and he was treated as a celebrity everywhere he went by everyone who knew him.

Charlie Reid played Free State League soccer, as it was known then, between 1929 and 1939. This was the equivalent of League of Ireland soccer now. He played in a forward position at inside left for notable Dublin-based league teams such as Brideville, Dolphin, Shamrock Rovers and St James's Gate. He played in the cup final for Shamrock Rovers against Cork in 1936 and scored the winning goal. He also won a Free State cup medal with St James's Gate, beating Dundalk in the final in 1938. He was selected to play for Ireland in 1931 against Spain in Barcelona, which they drew 1-1, and the following year he scored one of the goals for the Free State League team which beat the Welsh league 2-0 in Dalymount Park. The English team Blackburn Rovers was interested in signing Charlie and his friend Peadar Gaskins, but leaving Ireland didn't appeal to either of them.

Instead, Charlie married Eileen Thompson and continued his soccer career in his native land. After the 1939 season he said farewell to League of Ireland soccer, and it was then that things started to go wrong. Charlie and Eileen had three children by this time, having moved from 22 Grantham Street, a rented house, to a house they purchased at 79 Windsor Terrace, Fairview. It broke his wife's heart when Charlie sold the house and, despite tears and pleas, moved for short periods of time to two other rented houses on the southside of Dublin, and finally, with Noel, Kitty and Charlie and all the trappings they could bring with them, moved into 18D Block, Iveagh Buildings, Patrick Street, where I was born.

When they moved into the flat they brought with them expensive furniture and cutlery, carpets, and a wardrobe that included fox furs. A babysitter was employed when they went out together. This lifestyle was to deteriorate as Charlie began to frequent the public houses on his own. His fame followed him into his drinking circles, where he held court to all who enjoyed washing down soccer, politics and the old days with plenty of Guinness.

As a child I was terrified if I heard him slouching up the last few concrete steps outside the door. Dragging his feet meant he was drunk, and that meant, most of the time, verbal warfare with Mam. On the occasions when he wasn't drinking, his footsteps were light and quick, so I just lay back happy and fell asleep. My dad never physically attacked any of us, but all the shouting and intimidation seemed to a child a frightening prelude to violence. I would always hope that Mam would say nothing to him when he came in full of drink, just let him be and maybe he would fall asleep in the armchair.

The problem was that when Dad was drinking he was spending money that was needed at home, and my mother couldn't keep quiet about that. He had already lost a good job with the Shell oil company and had gone into the taxi business. I couldn't understand why he was causing so much hurt, when none of us did any wrong against him. I remember thinking, 'Why can't he be like my Uncle Leo?', who was my Auntie Annie's husband and lived across the landing from us. Uncle Leo was kind and warm and had time to talk to us, and I thought he would make a lovely daddy. Why couldn't my dad be like him, and then everything would be great.

I had no idea how to approach my dad or his problem. He never held conversations with us, we couldn't really communicate with him. He was someone who seemed to come and go and made me frightened going to bed in case it was going to be one of those nights. Sometimes he would go missing for days as if he didn't want to come home. He was a big man and I remember when he couldn't get into the flat one night, he broke open the heavy door with his shoulder. Another night when things got out of control my mother sent Charlie Junior running to get the police. It was about one in the morning and we were standing shaking with fear when they arrived. I can still remember these two huge men bending their heads coming through a six-foot-plus door. They dwarfed my dad who was six foot tall himself and demanded to know what he was doing frightening these children. 'You have a good wife and family, what's your problem?' they asked. I heard one policeman ask Mam if she wanted them to take him away and lock him up for the night. This was music to my ears, he was going away, now there would be peace and I could go back to bed. This very young child was hoping never to see her father again. I couldn't believe it when Mam said, 'No, I just wanted to frighten him.' The police left, telling her that she'd better be sure, because if there was any more trouble there would be no use sending for them.

Childishly, I used to ask God if he would take him, not to hurt him or anything, just take him up to Heaven and keep him there. He didn't go to Heaven, but at least he went off the drink for periods of sometimes up to five months. It was during one of these periods that he got a job driving a van for a seafood shop. These were rare happy moments when Dad was home regularly, and sober. We had a feast of seafood and there was great excitement when he'd bring home lobsters and prawns. The lobsters were alive and he used to chase us with them as we ran screaming around the flat. Mam would put on a huge pot of boiling water and we'd peep from a safe distance as Dad put the lobsters into the water. He would also bring home a hare or a rabbit, which Mam would clean out and prepare. We were treated to hare soup for starters, followed by lobster and prawns — I mean, where would you get it? All this was too good to last, and we were always waiting for the night when he wouldn't come home. One night he didn't come home, he was back on the drink, and he lost his seafood job. We had experienced a rare happy time with our dad, when he was a totally different person, but when the honeymoon was over, it was back to a nightmare on Patrick Street.

During all this, Mam was a tower of strength and it was she who kept the family together. She had marvellous patience, cooking meals for him and leaving them simmering for hours, waiting for him to come home, and on more than one occasion seeing them smashed against the wall in a fit of drunken temper. It didn't seem to bother her and to me it seemed that all these tribulations rolled off her like jam down wallpaper. She must have loved him very much to put up with this sort of behaviour all through the years. Mam was an attractive woman and I'm sure she missed being taken out socially by her husband. Instead she socialised only with close friends, and they were married couples, with her being the odd one out.

Sometimes her friends would come up to the flat on a Sunday night for a few drinks and a sing-song. For myself, Beatrice, Robert and Patrick, these Sunday nights were a great treat, when we were allowed to stay up late to be 'waiters' to our guests. Robert was undoubtedly the evenings' 'star turn'. He had everyone in stitches as he put everything he had into Al Jolson's 'Mammy' and 'California, Here I Come'. With eyes closed and on his knees, he drew thunderous applause from the small but very appreciative audience. If Robert had been gifted with a voice to match his antics he would have been a sensation on the cabaret circuit in later life. By contrast, Patrick was very shy and contented himself with sharing the task of going to the kitchen to get a bottle of porter from one of the brown paper bags when the need arose. At five years of age and the baby of the family, he was delighted with the responsibility he was given in collecting all the bottle corks discarded by people who had more important things on their minds. We were never allowed to bring a bottle of spirits from the kitchen in case we might drop it. I don't think cutting an artery would cause as much distress as the sound of a ten-year-old bottle of Jameson hitting the floor. Beatrice was always the culprit when it came to 'setting up' one of the adults with a request for them to sing a particular song that would send us kids into hysterical titters.

Mr and Mrs John Brocklebank and Larry and Maureen Rowantree were regulars at these get-togethers, as were Auntie Annie and Uncle Leo, and they always gave us kids a few bob before they left. As the beer and whiskey flowed, inhibitions were forgotten, and then the singing started. The songs of such greats as Perry Como, Guy Mitchell, Frank Sinatra and Vera Lynn were murdered, I mean rendered, and we had a great giggle at some of the facial expressions and sounds coming from these extremely happy vocalists. I learned quite a few new songs listening at these sessions, but there was one song I never learned the words to, and that was 'The Old Refrain'. Mam knew the song, it was her party piece, but when she came to the part that went 'It was my mother taught me how to sing', she always broke down and cried. There was never a dry eye in the house at this moment — luckily they had a few drinks to console them.

My dad wasn't usually at these small gatherings, but when he did arrive, I hid. He used to take over the place, standing with his back to the fire, and on a whim, shout for me to sing a song. He'd push me into the middle of the room and I would be forced to sing. I hated this, and even now, my pet hate is to be asked to sing at a party.

Things must have been at a particularly low ebb when Mam decided, or was advised, to seek legal advice. Herman Good's solicitor's office in Dawson Street, with me in tow, was my mother's port of call. She said she was just getting a solicitor's letter to frighten my dad. I told her it was a waste of time, he wouldn't be frightened, he knew all about these things, nothing would frighten him.

'I'll be with you in a minute, Mrs Reid,' greeted Mr Good, as he asked her to take a seat while he retreated into his office. Just then the door we had come in through burst open and this man in a trenchcoat, his belly sticking out, half jarred, hair all over the place, came in. 'Where's Herman, I have to see Herman,' he said, as he brushed right past us into the solicitor's office. 'How are you, Brendan,' said Mr Good, and in the same breath said smilingly, 'You don't mind waiting a moment, Mrs Reid?'

The man who barged into the office reminded me of my dad and I thought, maybe they're all over here. Mam turned to me and said, 'That's Brendan Behan.' I didn't know who Brendan Behan was, and judging by the cut of him I didn't want to know either. I wondered what he might look like if he were sober, because I had noticed that people's faces and attitudes changed completely when they were drunk. My dad looked like, and walked like, John Wayne when he had a lot of drink on him, and this was the reason I didn't like any of the 'Duke's' movies.

Mam got her advice, or whatever, from Herman Good, but it didn't make any difference to my dad. He continued to drink, missed most family social occasions, including weddings, communions, confirmations, and by his uncaring absence, lost his children. Even in his final years when he contracted Alzheimer's disease, we didn't know what to say to him, we still didn't know him, and still couldn't help him, except just to be with him in his last hours.

This was a child's eye view of the hopes and fears, the ups and downs, the day-to-day uncertainties of living in a home hit by the evil of alcohol abuse. It was by no means all doom and gloom as I will point out later, and no, I am not dishonouring my father. None of us have all the answers, but we can find a few together if we have the courage to share our experiences openly.

For whom the balls toll

When my mother was really stuck for a few bob there was no present like the time. The old reliable clock that existed before I was born, has survived the passage of time, travel, wars and pawnshops and still sits proudly on the sideboard in my mother's middle room in 18D. People know about time, travel and wars, but pawnshops know about people, what stories they could tell. They are now fading from major involvement in inner-city life, but I remember when they were a lifebuoy in the choppy seas of financial survival. As far as we were concerned, they were only used in times of emergency, and I could see nothing wrong with that.

Maybe because it was not done on a regular basis or perhaps for some other reason, the simple matter of going to the pawnshop was turned into something not unlike a chapter from a Frederick Forsythe spy novel. 'Don't use the bus-stop across the road, instead, walk up Nicholas Street to Christ Church and get the bus there where no one will see you,' Mam would tell me. 'Why walk two hundred yards when I can go across the road?' I would enquire, 'this clock is heavy, and besides, no one will know I am going to the pawnshop.' 'They probably would,' she'd say, 'do what you're told.'

The 54 bus went past our door in Patrick Street, right through town and up the North Strand towards its northside terminus in Killester. There was a bus-stop right beside the pawnshop, on the North Strand, and I'd say that when the three big brass balls came into view, I wasn't the only one standing up to get off with a parcel in their hands on a Monday.

The clock was well wrapped-up in a brown paper bag and put in a carrier bag and I was told to take my time and for God's sake don't let it fall. It certainly was a lovely clock, and efficient too, every fifteen minutes on the dot filling the whole flat with a gong. The pendulum was taken out, wrapped in newspaper, and put back inside, before the journey to its temporary home.

Apart from protecting it from being knocked about, the pendulum was wrapped for another reason. I wasn't the only one in my family to bring the clock across town and it never happened to me, but at one stage, on the fifteen-minute stroke, sitting in the bus, the gongs turned Kitty's pink cheeks to rosy red. I actually didn't care who knew I was going to the pawn, and it was no problem to me going back on Saturday to redeem our time-keeper.

My father's good suit was much lighter and less likely to embarrass you at the wrong moment, but it was a more risky operation. He never knew his suit was pawned occasionally, and it would just have to be back on Friday night in case he needed it at the weekend. We got more for the clock than the suit, so the suit was missing less often and the risk factor lessened.

Mam never told Dad about pawnshops because if he knew he probably would have pawned his suit and maybe everything else worth anything, drink the money and never redeem them. No, you couldn't tell him what was going on, or everything would vanish — we'd be walking around naked.

I could laugh things off pretty easily and saw the humour in situations that were supposed to be taken seriously. I still laugh when I think of the next episode. I got great amusement out of its conclusion, but what led up to it wasn't so funny. You've heard of people who are in trouble being described as 'up to their necks in hot water'. I was one of those unfortunate people who were up to their necks in hot water while they were actually asleep. I'm referring to the art of bed-wetting at which my sister Beatrice was a past master.

The two of us slept in a big four-foot-six bed and I had the uncomfortable honour of lying in my own Jacuzzi, with an endless supply of hot water provided by Beatrice. I slept near the wall and, despite practically climbing it, I couldn't get away from the flood. We never wore nightdresses, just a little 'above the bum' vest which absorbed the torrent up to its neck. I instinctively knew when she wanted to go — I could have gone for her myself, if I could. She used to lie in it and I'd say 'Why didn't you get out?', as I tried to find a dry spot near the wall. Even though the toilet was just twenty feet away, the only thing dry above or below the bed was the po under it, which was also ignored. The mattress was protected with an oil-sheet, but over the years the pee crept in under it like, I suppose, the opposite to rising damp, but the same effect.

Trying to dry the sheets and mattress wasn't easy for my mam, particularly in the winter time. Sometimes she'd send the sheets to the laundry, but most times they were hung up in front of the fire. 'Don't bring anyone in there,' she'd plead, if she thought we were expecting visitors. On a real fine day she'd open all the windows, and with the mattress standing sideways against the wall and the sheets hanging up, she'd let a healthy breeze whistle through, like in a sanatorium.

As time passed it was obvious that the mattress's days were numbered, with a hole eaten away in the centre. The straw-like stuffing was replaced with newspapers, packed in to fill up the hole. It had decayed so much that the springs caved in, and when I jumped into bed one night I went through it, my bum actually hitting the floor. I was left as if I had fallen backwards into a toilet with only my head, arms and feet sticking out. I had to be pulled out roaring my head off, and it was then that the decision was made — it had to go. My eldest brother, Noel, who was a very quiet, inoffensive and religious chap, was training to be a carpenter at the time and he very patiently did a stop-gap job with a piece of wood to tide us over.

Buying a new mattress was inevitable and not a problem. Now! we had to get rid of the old one, but how. A meeting was called and a committee comprising my mother, Noel and Charlie Junior formed.

'Why not have it collected?' — 'No! I'd be ashamed of my life.'

'Put it in a bag and . . .' — 'No bag would be big enough.'

'Cut it into pieces!' Noel was patient but he valued his saw and his sanity too much to go down that road.

'Throw it down into the Bayno yard!' — 'Be serious, this is no joking matter.'

'Roll it up and leave it around the corner!' — No, that was out, Mam would rather we got together and ate it, than have any neighbours knowing whose mattress it was.

'If we leave it here long enough it will walk out on its own.' No comment.

Come to think of it, I never did see a mattress left out for the binmen, maybe people did eat them.

However, our mattress was still standing sideways in the bedroom, defying us. Looking at it, I thought the patterns around the hole in the middle were quite attractive. In one way, they had a sort of sunburst effect, and in another, they looked like the scorched beard around the mouth of a man who smoked eighty cigarettes a day, but altogether I would describe the whole thing as a cross between modern art and a Pee-casso.

At last a decision was made — it was to be rolled up and tied tightly with twine and dumped into the 'Owler'. Don't ask me where the name came from but the 'Owler' was a piece of wasteground facing our flats. The minor details we had overlooked were that we lived sixty-eight steps up above one of the busiest streets in Dublin and the 'Owler' was fenced in by an eight-foot-high wall, with barbed wire on top curving out towards the path. Somehow, the Owler was to be the graveyard of the mattress.

The plan went like this. My mother was to oversee the operation, watching from the top window. Someone else, possibly Robert, who turned everything into fun and was a bigger giggler than I, would go down and watch from the hall door in the street. The things to watch out for were: people opening doors on any of the landings or someone coming in late through the hall door. All this was to be done about one o'clock in the morning and under the cover of darkness, except for street lighting of course. On an all-clear signal, Noel and Charlie were to dash across the road, having allowed for a break in the traffic, and while they were still running, with one big hoosh, throw the mattress over the wall and the wire into the Owler.

Preparations for the D-Day landings couldn't have caused General Eisenhower as much consternation as this operation caused my mother, who was worried sick looking out of the top window. 'Do it quick,' was her last instruction as her two brave secret agents started down the landing as if they were stealing the crown jewels. I don't know where Beatrice was, but at a guess I'd say she was working on the next mattress, drinking tea in the kitchen.

Everything went smoothly, the sentries did their jobs well, and with the first break in the traffic, Noel and Charlie charged across the road and with one movement together gave a mighty throw upwards. Mam didn't mind if a passing motorist saw this — he or she might even think it was a body being dumped, but as long as they didn't know whose mattress it was, she didn't care.

The boys had the height right but were a bit short on distance as our plan became unstuck, or should I say, stuck. The obstinate mattress gave us the two fingers, and Mam, watching from the window, had a near stroke as it sat on top of the barbed wire, as proud as an oil painting in an art gallery. Mam turned into a raving lunatic. 'I knew it wouldn't work, I have to do everything myself,' she screamed as the boys returned red-faced and panting to the flat. As far as she was concerned, our dark secret was plonked on display in the middle of Patrick Street for everyone to see.

Everyone from our neighbourhood going to Mass the next day could see the spectacle, including Mam, who passed it off with an unconcerned innocent look that said, 'I wonder who put that there.'

Jacob's ladder

'**D**id you feel that?' I said to the girl beside me. 'What?' she replied. I just left it at that, she obviously didn't feel this drenching, as if inwardly soaked in something from head to toe. I can still remember how strongly I felt it and how definite it was, coming just after Archbishop McQuaid told about six hundred of us children in Westland Row church that we were now soldiers in Christ's army and the Holy Spirit had come upon us. Mary was the name I had chosen, bringing my full title to Eileen Patricia Mary Reid on Confirmation day.

On this wonderful occasion when I renewed my baptismal vows and confirmed that I was a follower of Christ, I was put at the edge of a row of children from our school. Sister Lorcan did this because I knew the Catechism off by heart and the bishop usually asked questions of those at either end of a line.

In our case it was the archbishop of Dublin asking the questions and, true to form, he asked me, at the end of the line, 'Who is the visible head of the Church?' Would you believe, I got it wrong, as I answered, 'Jesus Christ is.' In fairness, his voice wasn't very clear, and I thought he said invisible head. 'No,' he said, but before he continued, I blurted out, 'Sorry, the Pope is.' He smiled at me, knowing that my second stab at it couldn't be wrong. 'That's right,' he said, and carried on.

I have very vivid memories of this great day, a day that made me feel very special and seemed to tell me that I was a big girl now and would have to start fending for myself. My mam had told me that I was too big to be rolling my dress up into my pants and doing cartwheels in the Bayno yard. My real childhood days were finally gone, days that I wouldn't change for anything, days that had their good times and bad, but were always tinged with hope, happiness and support. I had learned the great lessons of never dwelling on troubles, and always believing that things would work out.

It was then I began to learn a few very useful crafts from my mother that would be helpful right through my adult life. Things like wallpapering and painting and making the Christmas pudding, tasks that seem simple in theory but difficult without practical experience. I always liked helping Mam with these chores and I still have the actual recipe for her original Christmas pudding. The list of ingredients would take a chapter in this book, lifting it would put your back out, and the taste — do yourself a favour and write to me for the recipe. The taste of the pudding was as unique as the sound of the bells of Christ Church Cathedral, which were heard all over the Liberties. They had a sound that was especially attractive on New Year's Eve night, when thousands of people gathered to shout, dance, drink, and sing along with the chimes. I especially liked the bells welcoming in the new year two days before my fourteenth birthday, because I was filled with the happy thought of leaving school — forever. I didn't walk up to celebrate with the crowd, we were never allowed to, in case the festivities were turned to trouble by some over-excited inebriated revellers.

When my birthday did come and I was told I had to wait until the end of the term to leave, I was bitterly disappointed. But when the summer holidays finally came I forgot completely about school. I had failed the Primary Certificate examination and now the only way forward was to find a job. My mam believed that education for girls was a waste of time, they didn't need it, after all they were going to get married. Apart from this piece of homemade philosophy, the few bob that a job would bring in would certainly not go astray.

My search for a job ended when Judy Robinson, a relation of ours on my father's side, who was forewoman in a clothes factory called Orrwear, was contacted. The factory made jeans, overalls, boiler suits and dungarees, mostly for the export market, on its ground floor, and had a knitwear section above that.

I cycled to Orrwear in Hill Street, via O'Connell Street and Parnell Street, tasting for the first time that proud moment of apparent independence when, after my first week working, I presented, unopened, to my mother, an envelope containing one pound and four shillings.

Standing at a table and cutting the loose threads hanging from boiler suits was my first assignment in Orrwear. After six months, Mrs Robinson put me on a felling machine and told me I was on piece-work. This meant I was paid according to the amount of work I got through. The felling machine stitched up jeans, and for so much per jean, boy did I stitch them up. Because I was under age, I was not taxed, so my enthusiasm brought my wages far in excess of the rest of my co-workers, who came within the tax net. When their average wage was £6 per week and I rowed in one week with a whopping £9 envelope, Mrs Robinson wanted to know how a mere novice could get through so much work and experienced girls couldn't. The girls took me aside and explained that for them it wasn't worth the effort to earn any more than £6 because the taxman was getting most of the extra money. They told me not to make any more than they were making, but I replied, 'Why should I do that?' I wanted to work and my mam was delighted with the windfall.

There was good work and bad work: the bad work involved heavy material, as in boiler suits, and the good work, light material, such as shorts. When I was put on 'good work', it turned out bad for me. Mrs Robinson decided to pick me for a team to work on a big order for men's shorts.

Working right beside me was a machinist who reminded me of Dilly Dreams, a comic-book character. She actually looked like her, right down to her wire glasses, red plaited hair and face full of freckles. She used to make me laugh, and one day she did something that had me in stitches. Mrs Robinson caught me laughing and when I wouldn't, or rather couldn't, stop, she took me into Mr Orr's office and complained that I was laughing at her. When he asked me was it true, I said no, but I couldn't tell him that I was laughing at someone else. I just couldn't help myself. The more serious people looked when they were angry, the more I laughed. Mr Orr didn't see the funny side of it and sacked me.

I thought, first the choir and now my job, maybe I should have my funnybone surgically removed. I hid the bad news from my mam for a couple of days, telling her we were slack. When I finally broke it to her she couldn't believe anyone could lose their job simply for laughing but, in tune with her character, she shrugged it off and said we'd look for another one. Luckily she wasn't depending on me to bring home the bacon. Noel, Kitty and Charlie Junior were doing their bit to keep the house together.

Noel was a carpenter with Cramptons, the building firm. He was the strong, steady, dependable type, and like a father to us. He was considerate and generous to a fault, and when he left to join the monastery at Mount Mellery, my mother was heartbroken. It must have been her tears and prayers that brought him home eventually, to the delight of herself and his future wife and sweetheart, May Conroy.

Kitty was working in Mulcahys, a stocking factory in New Street, and being a very good worker brought home substantial wages. She handed all her earnings to my mam, and with equal dedication put her energy into the housework. Kitty used to mind us as small children and later she developed into a natural beauty with an hour-glass figure and shiny, chin-length wavy hair. When she went dancing in her lovely ballet-length dresses, she looked like a filmstar. Standing beside her I looked like a Russian farm worker.

Charlie was working with wood, as Noel was, but the significant thing about Charlie was that after he was born, Mam was advised not to have any more children. This I hasten to add was no reflection on Charlie, but referred to a complication that had developed with my mother's health. If Mam had taken heed of medical advice, I would not have been born, and as it was, I didn't arrive until a full six years later. Had she been in perfect health I probably would have been born years earlier and maybe never have been in a showband or never have been asked to write this book. But I suppose everyone could philosophise like this.

I soon joined my hardworking brothers and sister in helping the family budget by getting a job as a felling machinist in O'Connors of Capel Street for about six months. After this, I went to a childrenswear factory in Westland Row, but that only lasted a few months also.

During these times I was adding a little to my wages thanks to a contact I made while I was working in Orrwear. Before my laughing debacle there, one of their mechanics, a chap called Jack Dodd, asked me if I would like to sing in one of the concerts he used to organise. He knew I could sing a bit, and when I obliged, this led me to another contact. A cousin of mine, Arthur Neven, was leaving a small band and he invited me to audition as his replacement. I did, and got the job, as well as ten shillings (fifty pence) per night, twice a week. I remember my first gig was in the Glenville Hall on the South Circular Road. Before long, my vocal exertions were earning me the princely sum of one pound ten shillings per night with this little group.

I was to join yet another band, and I thought maybe Mam was right about me always joining things. The Melodymakers were the last band I joined before the Cadets came along. Billy Boyle, my old dancing partner from the Flanagan school, was singing with the Melodymakers and I was delighted to team up with him again. A present neighbour and friend of mine, Bobby Moore, was also in the band. We travelled further afield than the other groups I had been in and sometimes we went to country parts. If we travelled over a hundred miles from Dublin we would get four pounds. This was great, except for the fact that, arriving home at four or five in the morning and then having to be in Jacob's biscuit factory for an eight o'clock start was hectic, even for a sixteen-year-old.

I had got a job in Jacob's through the influence of Beatrice, who was already working there. Beatrice, a year younger, was a good dependable worker, and I suppose they thought, if I was anything like my sister, I would be OK.

I was delighted when I first started working in Jacob's, loving it straight away. I was employed in the stock department on the first floor, getting orders ready to be despatched to customers all over Ireland. I and a girl called Ann Cooney, a lovely looking girl who reminded me of Gina Lollabrigida, were given the job of going around the various biscuit sections with a four-wheeled trolley and an order sheet to fill. We would simply collect all the different types of biscuits that were needed to complete the order and stack them on the trolley. Then we would wheel it across a closed-in bridge, which spanned Bishop Street below and connected our stock department with the despatch department, which was in a completely different building. Here the orders were checked and then sent down in lifts to waiting trucks. Although the factory was huge, there weren't many people working in our section, which suited me fine. The work wasn't too strenuous so I had plenty of energy left for a little night life.

From the time I and my friends from Patrick Street and Bride Street flats first started dancing in Tír na nÓg, we stayed together, always going to whatever dancehall was fashionable at the time, as one big happy group. For those who are stupid like me, Tír na nÓg, loosely translated, means 'Land of the Young'. This hall, which specialised in *céilí* and old time dancing, was situated off Grafton Street just a leisurely walk from the flats. The Tommy Delaney *céilí* band was there regularly every Wednesday night. Tommy played set-dances to sweep us off our feet, and then vocalist Peter Coogan would provide a complete change of mood. Peter's calm, soothing voice was designed to bring lovers together, and it played its part in uniting couples who are still united today.

There was a great atmosphere in Tír na nÓg, everyone knew each other and all the patrons were very well groomed, hoping to attract the attentions of whoever they were 'chasing'. It was a meeting place for teenagers, and with the admission price at one shilling, it was great value. I, along with my sister Beatrice, Betty O'Rourke, Maura Duffy, Maureen Scanlan, Patty Little and many more, never missed Wednesday nights, and some even met their future husbands there.

Before or after the dance, the Palm Grove in Grafton Street was a popular spot for an ice-cream treat and a chat. Their Melancholy Babies and Knickerbocker Glories were absolutely delicious. My mam used to send Charlie Junior down to the Palm Grove on a Sunday to get three of these huge tubs, about nine inches tall, packed with fruit and ice-cream as well as fresh cream. At one shilling and three pence each, they were as dear as the admission to the dance, but they were well worth it.

Eating these ice-creams didn't seem to do the figures of such beauties as Patty Little and Betty O'Rourke much harm. Sporting skinny little waists, taffeta dresses, pink lipstick, nylon stockings, beautiful hair and facial features, they spent time on themselves, and it showed. The boys were mad about these two girls and would do anything to get to dance with them. By contrast, I was the 'rough and ready, let's have fun', tomboy type. At that time all my spare moments were spent swimming, so there were some Wednesdays when I would go directly from swimming to the dance. This resulted in me walking into Tír na nÓg with short pin-permed hair still wet, below the knees floral dress, short white socks, no make-up, face scaldy red, looking like Heidi in a dairy product advertisement.

A close friend asked me would I not try wearing nylons. I tried them but didn't like the restricted feeling they gave me. I went to the dances for the lively company, and to have fun, and do an innocent bit of flirting like everybody else, and if anyone had said they had a problem with my appearance, I probably would have replied, 'Frankly, my dear, I don't give a damn.'

On one occasion I did row in with the fashion of the times. Flouncey skirts were all the go, and in order to get a skirt to stand out more, wire hoops were inserted into the hem of an underskirt. The homemade job I did on the bottom of my skirt worked out fine until I had finished my first dance. Spotting a free space on a long bench-seat near the bandstand, I went over and sat down. As the back of the wire hoop hit the seat, the front part, carrying my skirt, shot up, blocking my vision of all who had a view of everything from my toes to my navel. In my desperation to rectify matters, I bent the front part of the wire into a figure of eight. A trip to the toilet saw me pulling the wire completely out, leaving the skirt as limp as an old cabbage leaf. Disposing of the wire, I emerged from the Ladies dressed like Cinderella before the ball.

I must have been a ten on the personality scale, because I was asked up to dance, but like most other girls, never by the chap I happened to be chasing at the time. To capture a moment with the boy of my dreams I'd simply wait for an 'Excuse Me' dance, tap the girl he was dancing with on the shoulder, and off I'd go, pretending to him that I had better things to be doing. Because I was a close friend of Patty Little and Betty O'Rourke, I used to be asked to dance by some of the 'Don Juans', a move they made just to get to the two lovelies. They'd ask me questions like 'Would you put a word in for me?' or 'Do you think I have a chance?'. When Pat Brady, dressed in a lovely cream jacket and matching ensemble, took me up to dance and then asked me to date him, I got a fright. Flirting was a bit of fun, but going on a date, this was serious. I said I'd like to, because I knew him well and he was a respectable chap, but I had to ask my mam and dad first. My dad asked me a thousand questions about Pat and finally gave the OK, provided I was home by ten o'clock. I told Mam we were going to the pictures and they wouldn't be finished till 10.45, but she just told me to go ahead and not to worry. I went with Pat for about three months and then we parted.

Tír na nÓg gave way to 'heavier', more exciting things in the form of a three-band session in the Olympia Ballroom in Pleasant Street, which was only a ten-minute walk from home. The three bands involved in this Tuesday-night extravaganza were the Jack Flahive Big Band, which included vocalist Marjorie McCormack who lived in Bride Street flats, pianist Noel Kelehan, of RTE and Eurovision fame, and drummer John Wadham, who taught half the country's drummers how to keep the neighbours awake. Jack's band kicked off the night and was followed by the fabulous Jimmy Compton Dixieland Jazz Band from the north of Ireland.

Then came the moment the packed ballroom was waiting for — the arrival of Dickie Rock and the Melochords. Amid screams of delight the queues for the ladies' toilets and the cloakrooms were abandoned as girls ran to get the best view of this new sensation. 'Spit on me Dickie' they roared, as the perspiration rolled down Mr Rock and company's faces. I never went near the stage, preferring to watch from the balcony, not realising that my future husband, Jimmy Day, was singing and playing the saxophone in the Melochords.

It was awful having to leave just a half hour into the band's programme, but I had to be home by eleven o'clock. I used to wait just long enough to hear my favourite song, the Everly Brothers' 'Let it be Me', sung by Jimmy and guitarist Brendan O'Connell. I had no problem retrieving my coat or getting to the toilet because everything on two legs was either dancing or bunched around the stage. Some girls were so eager not to miss anything, that they didn't queue for the cloakroom, but instead rolled up their coats and stacked them one above the other in the ladies' toilet, alongside the wall. I remember one Tuesday night the toilets overflowed, and when I happened to go in, the coats of these unfortunate owners, not only had toppled onto the wet floor, but were being trampled into the ground.

Every time I reluctantly left the Olympic Ballroom to get home, I thought how wonderful it would be to sing in a band like that. This I knew was just a dream, and tomorrow I would be back pushing a trolley across the bridge in Jacob's factory.

It is said that ignorance poisons people and I'm sure poisoning is very painful, which brings me to the painful subject of buying and wearing my first bra. What should have been a simple straightforward operation, through my ignorance turned into absolute torture. When I decided it was time for obvious reasons to purchase my first bra, I had no idea that the usual way to go about it was to be measured first. Little things like all-round back measurements and cups ranging from size A to double D, never entered my head as I walked into Cassidys and just asked for a bra. When the assistant enquired as to what size I was, I said I didn't know. Being very well endowed, I should have known that the high-fashion whirl bra with its cone shape and pointed top would be the last thing to lift and separate what I had. I was immediately attracted to this dainty, very feminine type of bra, and I bought one without even looking at the size. When I got home and Operation Cover-up began, I was pleased that I could fasten it at the back and the all-round size was OK. However, what was happening up front was another matter, as I wrestled with a task identical to putting a melon into an eggcup. No matter what manoeuvres I tried, nine-tenths of what was supposed to be inside was very plainly outside. With no busts in the cups, when the straps were fastened everything was squashed up against me. The weight of my breasts were too much for the shoulder straps, resulting in the taut straps digging a painful groove into both my shoulders. Taking the bra off at night, I groaned in pain as I pulled the straps out of their painful dug-outs, leaving raw red marks. When I drew Mam's attention to all this, she didn't even make a comment. For years afterwards, I just carried on like this, in ignorance of some of life's intimate personal details, simply because those closest to me, who possessed such information, wouldn't be 'caught dead' discussing sex, underclothes, personal hygiene or any other unmentionable topics.

Apart from pointed bras, I was later to have a problem with pointed shoes, when the height of fashion was attained by squeezing five toes into a space reserved for three. These shoes were a must for me when I started appearing on stage and caused permanent deformation of my toes and feet. To this day I have groovy shoulder blades and inseparable toes as a legacy to keeping up appearances. Oh, the agony of vanity!

The chain of events that took me into the Cadets show-band, which was an augmented version of the Melochords, kicked off in a most unusual way. It was through playing the game that brought my father to sporting prominence, that I got my chance at big-time entertainment. A seven-a-side interdepartmental ladies' soccer tournament was organised by Jacob's every year. Because I wasn't working there long enough, I thought I wouldn't get a place on the team. Being very eager to play, I asked the forewoman, Mrs Nagle, to keep me in mind if one of the selected squad got sick. I got on the team and played full back, never leaving my spot in front of the goalkeeper. The stamina I built up swimming and the speed I learned in the Bayno yard paid off. The girls up front did their jobs well, no one cracked our defence and we won the tournament.

A dance and prizegiving ceremony was held in Jacob's recreation hall, and one of the top bands in Dublin, the Blue Clavons, was hired to provide the music. This band included three brothers, John, Kevin and Harry Hardy. I had never heard them before and was pleasantly surprised, as they were very good. Some of the girls asked the band to let me sing a song with them. Kevin Hardy explained that it was not the band's policy to call singers from an audience, but they would make an exception, seeing as I was part of the winning team. After singing five songs Kevin told me I was very good and would like to help me with my career if he could. I went to see the Blue Clavons in the CYMS in Harrington Street and sat to the side listening to the music. The vocalists were Jim O'Connor and Christy Grace, and I was introduced by Kevin to his brother John, who was the band's leader.

John was a wonderfully helpful person and he gave me information about a band that was being formed at that time. He explained that this band would go further in the music business than his own and it was backed by big management. The band, later to be named the Cadets, was looking for a drummer, keyboard player and vocalist, and auditions were to be held in the Town and Country Club on Parnell Square. On John's advice I agreed to go to the auditions. In fact, he set my audition up and drove me there himself. What hit me when I walked in was that I seemed to be the only female in the whole place. Future RTE producer Ian McGarry was there, and being a fabulous drummer he was to get the job on 'skins'. After belting out Shirley Bassey's 'I Reach for the Stars' and an old reliable 'Stupid Cupid', I was thanked for coming and I left.

The following Wednesday night I went to the CYMS, and while listening to the music I was told that someone wanted to speak to me in the kitchen. When I got to the kitchen I was greeted by two gentlemen, a Mr Tom Costelloe and a Mr Pat Murphy. Mr Costelloe explained that he would shortly be managing a newly formed band and he asked me if I would be interested in joining. As well as meeting Pat Murphy at the auditions, he had heard me singing with the Melodymakers, and it was Pat who had convinced him that I was right for the band. Tom Costelloe, who was involved in the promotional side of the music business, told me that Pat, who played harmonica, was to be the leader of the band, and my starting wage would be twenty-seven pounds a week. I at once said I was interested, and with that we all went upstairs to meet some other members of the future Cadets showband. I remember Jimmy, Brendan O'Connell and Noel McGann were on the balcony, but when Tom Costelloe introduced me to them, they didn't seem overjoyed to meet me. I was invited to a rehearsal in the Crystal Ballroom, but I felt I was not wanted by some of the band, including Jimmy. It was nothing personal, they probably didn't want the hassle of a female among them, preferring a hip-swinging male sex symbol to front the line-up.

Pat Murphy wanted everything to be different, so to get away from the usual mohair suits, he decided to dress the band in a uniform. Everything from postmen to convicts was considered, but he finally settled for naval uniforms, complete with authentic caps and badges, and the name Cadets. We made a 'dry run' under the name of the Admirals in what is now the Garda Club in Harrington Street, on St Stephen's night 1961, just to feel out the reaction to our show. The band, with Ian McGarry on drums, Frank Nolan, keyboard, Noel McGann, bass, Brendan O'Connell, guitar, Noel Milner, trumpet player, who was replaced by Paddy Burns very shortly afterwards, Jas Fagan, trombone, Jimmy Day, tenor, saxophone, yours truly lead vocalist and Pat Murphy on harmonica, went a storm, and then it was decided to do a few 'gigs' in the country under the name of the Cadets just to sharpen us up for an assault on the 'Big Smoke'.

Although the band went very well, I was unhappy and disappointed because, out of a two-and-a-half-hour programme, I sang just a handful of songs, and I still felt I was going to be dumped. Apart from Pat Murphy, I did have a couple of other allies, one of which was a very quiet lovely lady called Kathleen 'Kotch' Clinch, who was appointed to be secretary of our fan club, and she supported my inclusion in the band. My other source of consolation was the driver of our minibus, Ignatius. 'Iggy', as we called him, used to leave me off last as we returned from our first few trips, and I tearfully confided in him regarding my future with the band. He told me not to worry, he would talk to Pat Murphy and he was sure everything would work out.

My fears were put to rest not by anyone connected with the band but by a chance meeting with a ballroom owner. Every Thursday night a really big band was featured in the Crystal Ballroom in Dublin. Bands like the Royal Showband, Mick Delahunty, Johnny Flynn and Johnny Quigley to name but a few were top draws. One Thursday night I went over to watch and met up with Pat and some of the Cadets. A man called Seamus Brown, who owned a ballroom in Lifford, County Donegal, happened to be there and was talking to Pat. We were due to appear in his ballroom the following Friday night and Pat was telling him about the problem with me and the rest of the group. Pat explained that it was easier to get a vocalist than replace part or all of the band. Mr Brown, however, explained that he could solve the problem for Pat, saying that if I was not with the band, he would cancel our engagement in his ballroom the following Friday. Pat put this new revelation to the members of our group who were there after the dance, and asked them to think about it. They did, and not liking to start off the band's career with cancellations, they agreed to carry on as we were. Whether their decision was made reluctantly or whether they were beginning to get used to me, I don't know, but either way I was here to stay. I said goodbye to Mr Knaggs, my manager in Jacob's, who was delighted for me and wished me well, and then it was full steam ahead to fame or failure.

Part Two

Anchors away

Although showbands on a grand scale came from the south of Ireland and brought their unique form of musical charisma across the border to the north, the very first Irish showband was actually formed in the north of Ireland itself. A trumpet player called Hugo Quinn from the Strabane area got a band together in 1952. He threw away the traditional music stands that orchestras used to read their scores, gathered round him a group of multi-talented musicians, and put on a breathtaking show. This first Irish showband was named the Clipper Carlton. The high-energy show featured every member of the band, each one impersonating different international stars of the time. They had the scene to themselves for a few years until a group of youngsters from Waterford hit the dancehalls with tremendous impact. They called themselves the Royal Showband, and their lead singer, Brendan Bowyer, was to be the sensation of Irish showbusiness. They were exactly what the younger dancer was looking for, and everywhere they appeared for the first time, the place was packed for their return. The north of Ireland responded with the great Johnny Quigley band, which had a lot of the Royal's non-stop, hard-hitting, energetic music. A demand for this type of dance-cum-show was created, the dancers were coming back, and the potential for generating big money was spotted. The floodgates were opened, with the south providing most of the really popular bands — Johnny Flynn from the west, the Dixielanders from the south, and Joe Dolan and the Drifters the most popular midlanders.

When we hit the scene, the competition was intense,

showbands were springing up like mushrooms, and big ballrooms were being built as fast as possible. There were eventually over eight hundred showbands in Ireland, and every one of them was striving to be different. Every gimmick in the book was tried. Flashy suits, with a band starting their show, say, in red suits and changing to yellow or green, or maybe someone dressing up in costume during a comedy sketch. No one stood still for a second, and even if you had two left feet you had to learn the deft little foot movements or side-to-side shuffle that was the trademark of showbands. Everyone in the band had to be very talented, singers would play instruments, and you could get a great instrumentalist who could sing as well as the lead vocalist. Variety had top priority and no 'dead weight' was carried.

Publicity was fiercely contested, even minibuses got bigger and flashier, with reclining aircraft seats, wardrobes and built-in record players, and no one in any possible doubt as to who travelled in these moving livingrooms. Huge coloured posters adorned the venues and public places, coloured photographs were handed out with abandon, and the insides of newspapers were packed with ads for coming showband attractions. Any band that was falling on hard times was often billed as appearing for the first time after a long, triumphant tour of half of Europe or South America.

We were not the only Dublin-based band at this time to start this musical adventure. A few familiar faces cropped up from the past, like Butch Moore who sang with the Blue Clavons and had joined the Kelly Brothers, Des and Johnny, and Paddy Cole in the Capital Showband. Dickie Rock turned up to front the newly formed Miami Showband. All over the country new names were appearing, like the Blue Aces and the Black Aces and the Premier Aces. The cards were stacked against us, but our ace in the hole was our officer-style naval uniforms, giving visual effect backed by a thumping good band. Our uniform consisted of a royal blue double-breasted jacket with gold braid on the arms, brass buttons adorned with anchors, epaulets with gold braid, brass chain around the shoulder, under the armpit and into the top breast pocket, white trousers with blue stripe, white shirt, pale yellow tie, cap with white top and badge, blue shoes with white trim. The Cadets were aptly named, because the whole set-up was very regimental — we were actually living out how we were dressed.

Although Brendan Bowyer was lead singer of the Royal, it was another member of the band who started showband singers on the recording trail. Tom Dunphy, the Royal's bass player, was the first man to have a record released in Ireland, when 'Come Down the Mountain Katey Daly' hit the music shops. Radio Éireann started Ireland's Top Ten, and the first Irish singer to make it into the Irish pop charts was Pat McGuigan with 'Hawaiian Wedding Song'. Pat's son Barry, who probably wasn't even born then, was later to become a world boxing champion. It was all happening, Ireland's biggest-ever music business was up and running. We knew it was going to be difficult to make it to the top, but apart from having faith in ourselves, we were in at the beginning and could grow with this new-born monster called the Irish showband.

Being a robust working-class girl, I never had any illusions about the glamorous side of my profession. The challenge was exciting and the work involved didn't cost me a thought. I could work round the clock at something I really liked and wouldn't call it work, my contented mind keeping my body going.

The first lesson I learned was that this showband business was not glamorous, it was indeed very hard work. They say that when the going gets tough, the tough get going. Well, this was tough, and after a few months on the road we really began to get going. We were doing six nights a week, travelling to the north, south-east and west of Ireland, and in the early years performing for five hours on stage. While most bands didn't start playing until the crowd began to come in, we blasted off bang on 9 pm. Pat Murphy's theory was, and he was right, that even if there was no one in the hall, we were to start playing anyway. Most of the dances then were from 9 pm to 2 am, and people would sit in their cars outside the ballroom from before nine o'clock, not making a move until they heard music. If they didn't like what they heard, it wouldn't be too late to drive, sometimes up to thirty miles, to another town, and hopefully a better band. So when we kicked off at 9 pm sharp with a couple of country or Dixieland numbers, moving in unison from side to side in our beautiful naval uniforms, the verdict was 'this will do us', and in they'd come. I always thought that the Cadets had a great mixture of music. I covered the songs of girls like Patsy Cline, Kitty Wells, Connie Francis, Dusty Springfield, Shirley Bassey, Lulu and even Cilla Black.

Paddy, Jas and Jimmy did some Dixieland jazz and Brendan on guitar 'twanged' out the hits of Hank Marvin and the Shadows. Frank occasionally used to play a classical number when he'd come across a good piano in some decent ballroom. Hermin's Hermits and Elvis were represented with great gusto by Paddy, while Noel with his soft country-style voice featured in Hank Locklin and Marty Robins' songs. Jimmy handled the Roy Orbison high notes with great effect and was joined by Brendan for some sweet Everly Brothers' duets, including the one I used to wait for on the balcony of the Olympic Ballroom, 'Let it be Me'. When I later heard a band called the Freshmen doing their superb impression of the American Beachboys, I put it on a par with Noel, Brendan and Jimmy's version of a Beatles' medley. To cap things off, we probably had the only featured harmonica player on the showband scene. When our leader Pat played 'Smoke Gets in Your Eyes', you could close your own and think you were listening to the great Larry Adler.

I loved singing in the band and would rather have lost a limb than have to give it up, but those ballrooms were something else. Those Dreamlands and Jetlands and Roselands were literally a huge floor surrounded by four walls and a roof. I came across very few that had hot water, toilet paper, towels or soap in the ladies' toilet, but they did have a sandwich bar they expected you to eat in. The rooms where the boys changed were a disgrace, without even a chair to sit on or a wall-hook to hang clothes. The floors were weeping with some white limey substance that soiled shoes and clothes alike. All the showbands spent a lot of money on the very best of clothes and then had to put plastic covers on the floor when they were changing to go on stage. In the winter the halls were freezing, and when the band's fee included a meal, all too often we would be greeted after hours on the road and facing a five-hour run on stage, with a slice of cold ham, a tomato and a piece of lettuce. The boys eventually rebelled and simply stopped at the nearest hotel or restaurant to the ballroom, had a good meal, gave the bill to Pat, and didn't mind who it upset.

Trying to freshen up and do my hair, which was in a beehive style and took about an hour to arrange, in a cold toilet, was an ordeal. When we travelled over the border into Northern Ireland, I found the attitude much more professional. The halls were heated, the toilets immaculate, the dressingrooms comfortable and the meals hot and substantial. Despite eating well, I lost three stones in weight in the first eight months I was in the band. When I went for medical advice to Dr John O'Connell, who later became a politician, he was shocked and advised me to give up the band for three months. I told him I couldn't give it up for twenty-four hours. 'When you collapse and are brought into hospital you'll have to give it up,' he said. Taking a bottle of Guinness every day was then suggested, but I said I didn't drink alcohol. My mam was angry with me and desperately worried, as was my sister Beatrice, who was singing in a band about twice a week herself.

The problem was that I was getting to bed most mornings at about 7 am, but would have to be up then at 1 pm to meet the minibus at three o'clock and start another cycle of sixteen hours' travelling and singing, before I would see my bed again. Mam and Beatrice used to pull me out of bed onto the floor. I couldn't wake up, so Mam would put a cold wet cloth on my face to get me to my feet. 'You'll have to give it up,' she'd shout, 'you're fading away to a skeleton.' I would reply, 'Don't you ever let me sleep it out, even if you have to kick me.' She never let me down, so at lunchtime I would walk around the flat like a zombie, not having the appetite to eat the big dinner she'd have for me. Beatrice couldn't understand how I kept going because the two or three gigs she was doing were getting her down. I fought my tiredness and battled on because I wanted the band life so much. It might have helped if I could have slept on the way home, but I couldn't. I used to sit in the front of the minibus with Pat, who was doing all the driving at that time, and talk to him for the entire journey.

I couldn't relax. I'd come off the stage on a permanent high, as if I was on drugs, so when I got home I simply collapsed into my bed. It took my body close to three years to adjust, but this hard training-ground toughened me for a very busy life later on, and thank God I still feel fit and well today. It's true I never drank alcohol while in the band, and neither did Pat Murphy or Jimmy. The rest of the boys were very moderate drinkers, and even if they had not been, the rule was two pints before a gig and that was it. There was absolutely no drugs used and I doubt if the band even knew what drugs looked like, let alone their effect.

Yes, things were strict, and just to give an example, I'll describe one incident that happened to us. We were delayed, for what reason I can't remember, in getting to a ballroom called Borderland in Muff, County Donegal, which was owned by a real gentleman called Jim McIvor. We arrived at 8.45 in a panic because the dance was to start at nine o'clock. Having no 'roadies' in those days, the boys had to unpack the minibus themselves, set up the sound system and back-line amps, and make a very quick change to get on stage. The ladies' toilet was where I had to get ready. My complicated beehive hairstyle, held up with dozens of clips and lacquer, was going to take some time. I was sharing a long mirror with girls who were fixing their make-up and chatting excitedly about the night ahead. The band had just started when a girl came into the toilets and told me I was wanted immediately on stage. I was only half way through doing my hair, so I couldn't go telling the girl I'd be out as soon as possible. Ten minutes later another girl came in with the same message. As I was putting the finishing touches to my hair, Pat barged into the Ladies and in front of everyone there, ordered me out of the toilets and onto the stage. He said if I didn't move immediately I would be sacked.

Apart from occasional unpleasant incidents like this, we were really and truly like a family. I was treated with respect, like a sister, by all the boys, and despite being in one another's hair six nights a week all year round, when it came to our two-week break, we all went on holidays together to the same location in Spain. The discipline in the band really suited me and I benefited from it. I heard about bands staying back after dances and having long drinking sessions, all chiefs with no Indians, and this would not have been to my liking at all. When we stayed over in hotels, and if we were not too tired, we'd have a game of cards, the boys would have a few beers and we'd enjoy ourselves.

The question of money always raises its head when people talk about showbusiness. Money was not a top priority when I joined the band, I just loved the singing and the excitement, and besides, I was always bad at handling money. We were not, as it was known then, a co-op band, that is, splitting the money in equal shares among the band members after paying a manager and leaving aside so much for other expenses. We signed a contract every so often and worked for a wage and occasional bonuses. Our wages ranged from thirty pounds to sixty pounds per week during the eight years the band was operating, and I remember getting a bonus of a hundred pounds from time to time. We actually worked on a couple of Christmas nights, which everyone except me consented to, for almost three times our nightly wage.

Everybody in the Cadets was paid exactly the same wages

throughout the band's existence. What we got was our own, our income tax was paid, as were expenses such as uniforms, transport, publicity, hotels, food, recording sessions, photographs and other things I knew nothing about. I don't know how other people found out what we were earning, I certainly told no one, but I was quizzed in a rather ridiculing way by a singer in another top showband which happened to be co-op. He was boasting about earning between one hundred and fifty pounds and as much as three hundred pounds a week, depending on the size of the crowds, and he informed me that he knew what I was being paid and that I was being 'ripped off'. I made no comment, not having his cheek to enquire what was left of his big money when all his expenses were paid. We were members of the Cadets, not the owners. The Cadets were formed and funded by Tom Costelloe in association with Pat Murphy, and as far as I was concerned it was not my business to know what the band cost. I negotiated a contract, signed it and got what I signed for, and despite being approached by another big management and offered much more money, we all preferred to stay with the Cadets. Our job was to put on a show, Tom's job was to sell it, keep it together and balance the budget, and Pat's job was to drive the minibus, collect fees, look after expenses on the road, and keep discipline in the band. We trusted our management and proved it by staying the full showband course with it, and what was very important, to me at least, was the lesson of having good discipline in whatever you are doing. I never begrudged those who set up their own co-operative band, put their own money and talent into it and took their chances. Lots of these musicians made extremely good money, went into business afterwards and are contented today. What really makes me sad is when I see how many alcoholics and broken homes this 'huge money' spawned. I wonder was it all worth it to these unfortunate fallen stars.

The hardest part of any band's career is actually getting the bookings to begin with — no one wants to take a chance on an unproven product. Selling any new product takes money, hard work, influence and confidence in it. Our manager Tom happened to be the manager of the Crystal Ballroom and knew quite a bit about the music industry. Although he had good connections and we got into the best venues, if we didn't produce the goods on stage and draw crowds, then we wouldn't get a return booking no matter how influential Tom was. So with nothing but raw talent and youthful enthusiasm during the whole of 1962, we got stuck into the task of making our presence felt. We just wanted people to hear us, so when we played to crowds that gathered spontaneously, like at festivals or holiday nights, it was a bonus and a worthwhile opportunity.

One such opportunity and a great shop window for bands was Tramore in County Waterford during the summer months. It was a popular holiday resort, particularly for Dubliners and especially in August. We got a booking to play for the first two weeks in August at the Atlantic Ballroom. I have some lovely memories of Tramore, where I saw the beginning of a new trend in dancing, met countless new friends, had an embarrassing experience and a lasting emotional one. During our two-week stay there we played some full nights ourselves, but also did two-band sessions with other showbands that were making big names for themselves.

Every band had a common enemy on these holiday sessions — the heat. One particular night was so hot that after the dance I saw our trumpet player, Paddy, squeeze the sleeve of his jacket and the perspiration poured out in big drops. During the dance I noticed that some teenagers near the stage, most of them from Dublin, were doing a strange new dance. They were standing in one spot, separately, and while shaking their bodies, their elbows were flapping like young birds trying to fly. The bouncers struggled through the huge crowds and put a stop to these 'weirdos' who were forming a 'dangerous new cult'. I had seen boys and girls separated for dancing too close, particularly in parish halls, in compliance with strict moral behaviour, and now that they were dancing separately, they were still in trouble. There's just no pleasing some people.

However, on that particular night in Tramore, the teenagers just waited until the bouncers went back to the front door and then they continued doing their thing. While we were putting every ounce of energy into doing our thing, the heat was getting to us. Our shirts were stuck to our backs, and perspiration running down onto already wet lips was producing difficulties for our brass section, not to mention some unavoidable 'bum' notes. There seemed to be water everywhere except inside us. My scalp was saturated and this started to have an effect on my twelve-inch-high beehive hairstyle, to the extent that, while I was dehydrating, my hair was disintegrating. Like ice-cream melting, it started to collapse. Bit by bit my crown was turning into a cap and there was nothing I could do about it. Pretty soon I was looking through a curtain of wet hair and clips, but everyone was so busy trying not to pass out, and keep cool, they paid little attention to my predicament.

Lucky stars

Although my hair collapsed in Tramore, something else was building up. It was my love for Jimmy Day, our saxophone player. When I joined the band first, I hated him because I thought he resented me being there and he would have the most influence in getting rid of me. As time went by, I knew his initial coolness was nothing personal, I began to like him, but I didn't know how he felt about me. There was the usual flirting, with girls fancying different members of the band, and I knew of one who fancied Jimmy a lot. She actually came down to Tramore that August weekend and asked me to 'fix her up' with Jimmy. She didn't know that I fancied Jimmy myself.

One evening I told Jimmy that this girl liked him a lot and he just turned to me and said, 'I don't fancy her, it's you I like.' When we showed our feelings openly it came as a bit of a bombshell. Pat Murphy said it wouldn't last, we were as different as chalk and cheese. I suppose the rest of the boys were anxious in case it would cause uneasiness in the band if we had tiffs or quarrelled. The worst scenario would have been if I became pregnant and had to leave the band, then the management would have got the old 'I told you so' and it would be the last time the Cadets would be seen with a girl singer.

Jimmy was very quiet, with an almost pious way of conducting himself, and was known in the band as 'the vicar'. To anyone who knew us well, it was like the mad hatter walking out with the dormouse. It was an unusual alliance, but it worked, and if we had any personal differences we kept them to ourselves. Jimmy would only get involved on my side when he thought it necessary, and then only on principles of band business. In all other matters I was left on my own.

Shortly after we started dating, Jimmy told me that he had met Dickie Rock coming out of Waltons' music store in North Frederick Street in Dublin. Dickie and Jimmy were old friends, having been in the Melochords together. Commenting on our relationship, he told Jimmy to ignore everybody, unusual partnerships are the most successful, and if you love each other, go for it. This flamboyant attitude was typical of Dickie, and although Jimmy's mind was already made up, he appreciated his vote of confidence.

While in Tramore, I remember Jimmy and I went for a drive outside the town. It was a beautiful day so we sat in a field and kissed and cuddled. We were so interested in each other that we didn't notice a few inquisitive cows coming over to investigate us. I'd never seen cows that close before and I was afraid they might bite me. Despite Jimmy's reassurance, I jumped up and ran. When we stayed over in hotels with the band, I slept alone, and the only time we got to kiss any way passionately was when he left me home after our free Monday night out together. Six nights a week on the road, the seventh going to the pictures or having a meal out, and then back on the road again. Most people would say that this would drive saints apart, but with the exception of a short cooling-off period, we stayed together.

Moving into 1963, the number of showbands must have doubled judging by the extra coaches on the road. Very few of the top twenty bands at that time had female vocalists. Some that come to mind are Kelly and the Nevada, a mixture of a Cork-born girl with a Dublin-based band. Eileen Kelly, who took the stage-name 'Kelly', is to this day a very good friend of mine. Tina and the Mexicans were a great young showband and Tina went on to represent Ireland in the Eurovision Song Contest. Terry Mahon sang with the Jim Farley Showband, which also featured Roly Daniels. The Hoedowners, who sported the talents of Irish Eurovision star

Seán Dunphy and the maestro himself, trumpeter Earl Gill, had the lovely Deirdre Wynne.

Baring their bottoms against their coach windows was a popular way of saying goodnight for a playful all-male showband, as they passed us on the road home, knowing we had a female on board. Ambushes were a frequent thing at one stage, with bands lying in wait in the dark and hurling raw eggs and flour at their rivals as they negotiated a bend. Dangerous? Yes! But you would have to be a little crazy to be in the business in the first place. We always had to be on the lookout for things like a musician dressed as a policeman who would send you on a detour, or an unfortunate bandsman who would be dumped out of his coach and left to hitch a lift in his nude, knowing that we would be along soon, all of course for my benefit and extra embarrassment for the hitch-hiker.

One night our headlights picked out a statue on top of a gate pillar leading up to a big house. The statue wasn't a stone lion or a bronze eagle, but a naked male showing off every muscle more effectively than Mr Universe. It was a bit far from Cork to be Joe McCarthy, Irish showbands' zaniest and most lovable character. I strongly suspected one of Dublin's musical lunatics, Dave Pennefeather, and if it was you Dave, I forgive you and promise never to print it.

From the Strand Ballroom in Portstewart to the Floral Hall and Romanos in Belfast, right across to the Pavesi Ballroom in Donegal and through the Reynolds Brothers' and the Associated Ballrooms chains, to the Eclipse dancehall in Ballyhaunis, County Mayo, back to the Atlantic Ballroom, Tramore, to the Majestic in Mallow, beyond that to the Las Vegas in Listowel, and back through far too many others to mention, to the cradle of the stars, the Crystal Ballroom in Dublin, we played them all. Tens of thousands of miles were clocked up on our two smartly decorated Opel Kadett station wagons which were purchased to facilitate north- and southside members of the band when we returned from gigs. Jimmy dropped the northsiders home and Pat drove those who lived on the southside.

73

While playing a venue in Belfast, we were heard by a representative of BBC television, who was so impressed that he invited us over to London to the *6.25* show. I remember singing 'Tell Him', a hit by a singer called Billie Davis, and meeting artists like Billy J Kramer and Eden Kane who were appearing on the same show. After the show, the band was offered a recording contract by Decca Records. Shortly after this, Jimmy and I recorded 'Hello Trouble' and 'Our First Quarrel' with an orchestra at Decca Studios. Although Tom Costelloe was our manager, an agreement was made that a very big English music promotion agency would represent us in the UK.

Things seemed to be moving nicely for us and continued to do so when our very powerful representatives in England got us a slot on the equivalent of today's *Top of the Pops*, a show called *Thank Your Lucky Stars*. This TV spectacular was the launching pad for many of the top artists who later dominated the British charts. The Rolling Stones were just starting off their careers when we met them on the set of *Lucky Stars*. Mick Jagger, the late Brian Jones and the rest of the Stones were dressed in single-breasted herringbone jackets and drainpipe trousers. Mick had silky natural blonde hair and was actually good-looking. When he started his unique body-jerking movements, we all thought he wasn't the full shilling, but speaking to him in the canteen during a break, I found him to be a perfect gentleman. He thought our uniforms were fantastic and was sorry the Rolling Stones didn't think of something like that themselves. Little did Mick know that exactly one year later, the Stones would have their first Number One in Britain with 'It's All Over Now'.

We performed 'Hello Trouble' on that July Saturday night in 1963, and when we arrived the following Tuesday night for an engagement in the Orpheus Ballroom in Belfast, we were in for a big surprise. The police were controlling the crowds of teenagers outside and we thought, this is all we need, there must be a mix-up in the bookings, and some cross-channel superstar is booked instead of us. When we drove up and it became obvious that we were the cause of all the excitement, we just couldn't believe it. That one appearance on *Thank Your Lucky Stars* had made the Cadets into a major attraction in the north of Ireland. Jim Aiken, who booked the band for the Orpheus, was delighted with our success, and Jim today is still doing great business promoting big international stars in Ireland. Because ninety per cent of the south of Ireland didn't get English television, we didn't capitalise on our appearance here as much as in the north.

I loved playing the ballrooms in the north of Ireland and made many great friends there, so when the serious troubles began about a year after I had left the band to get married, I felt deeply sorry for all the ordinary innocent people there. We entertained Protestants and Catholics alike and found them all the most friendly, fun loving, helpful people you could meet anywhere. Some of them invited us back to their homes after the dance, and on occasions we accepted the invitation for a cup of tea and a chat with their families. I never knew whether they were Catholics or Protestants and I didn't care. None of these people deserved the tragic sufferings they had to endure, and I sincerely hope that permanent peace will be found, for all of us to share and enjoy.

Apart from Borderland in Muff, County Donegal, and the Orpheus in Belfast, some of the other halls I liked were the Floral Hall and Romanos in Belfast and Milanos in Bangor. There was always a relief band which played for the first part of the dance in Belfast, and it was through a lady singer in one of these bands that I was enlightened in the art of make-up. I thank her for introducing me to the lip pencil. I had never even heard of these things before and I was so impressed with its results that I use exactly the same type today. I learned a lot about fashion and make-up from the girls in the north, and during our stopovers in Belfast I'd look forward to a visit to the C&A store where I could buy clothes that weren't available in Dublin. Some of the boys in the band also bought trendy gear in the north, including Willie Devey who replaced Ian McGarry on drums, and Gerry Hayes who took Frank Nolan's place on keyboard. Ian and Frank went on to do other things, with Ian later becoming an RTE television producer. Willie and Gerry were former members of the Melochords, so they fitted in very nicely with our set-up.

There were no songwriters on the showband scene, we all did covers of proven songs, and this was a big drawback when tackling the international market. If you could write your own hit songs, it would give you much better bargaining power when it came to doing deals with music agencies.

The greatest example of this in the sixties and possibly in the entire history of pop music was displayed by a group we met in Dublin on 7 November 1963 — the famous Beatles. They did two shows in the Adelphi Cinema and caused a riot. Hundreds of police tried to keep order and many people were hurt and quite a few arrested. The fab four were staying in the Gresham Hotel in O'Connell Street and our manager Tom Costelloe arranged for us to meet them. As I waited in the corridor outside the room where they were resting, accompanied by Tom, Pat and a couple of the Cadets' members, a legion of screaming Beatles' fans were outside and would have killed to be in my shoes.

When John Lennon and Paul McCartney came out of their room, we were introduced as a major force in the Irish music scene, who dressed in naval uniforms and were noted for our interpretation of Beatles' hits. Paul was very natural and friendly and seemed unaffected by his success. He put his arm around me for the photograph session and gave me a playful squeeze. He was interested in all we were saying and was happy with his own good fortune. John Lennon was the opposite, being down in the mouth and with that 'What am I doing here with these people?' look on his face. When he heard that we were doing the Beatles' hits on stage, he quickly said it was all right to perform them, but we couldn't record them. He seemed to think someone might take something from him, and he was a bit possessive about what he had achieved. The boys in the Cadets didn't like him either, but we were glad of the opportunity to talk to the most famous showbusiness people we would ever meet. Ringo Starr and George Harrison didn't come out of their room, but John and Paul did enough talking for them all.

A welcome change from the norm was when we toured with the famous Johnny Cash and June Carter and their band. Coming from America, the Irish climate didn't suit poor Johnny, who had the flu during the entire tour and felt miserable. It was during the month of October, and while we didn't think it was unusually cold, the American entourage couldn't keep themselves warm. While staying in a hotel in Galway, I remember going to June Carter's room to collect some photographs she promised me, and when she opened the door I was hit by this incredible heat. She must have had heaters on all over the place and she said she still wasn't warm. That same morning Johnny came down to breakfast and promptly ordered mashed potatoes and sausages. The staff told him that he could have this at lunchtime, when they were prepared and on the menu. Apparently in the southern states of America, you could get turkey for breakfast if you wanted it, so Mr Cash insisted on his bangers and mash. He waited until they were cooked, and since there were no microwaves then, it took quite a while. When we were getting up from the table, after our cornflakes and boiled eggs, Johnny was getting stuck into a big plateful of mashed potatoes and about half a dozen sausages. We built up a very good relationship with Johnny and June during their stay in Ireland, and the highlight of our tour together was a concert in the National Stadium in Dublin. The concert was on a Saturday night, 19 October 1963, and featured a group called the Stellas, who opened the show along with the Cadets, with Johnny, June and his American band finishing off the evening. I'm glad to see that these two very likable Americans are still going strong in the entertainment business today.

Another person who certainly lasted the pace through the years is the legendary broadcaster, Gay Byrne. We met Gay for the first time when he was hosting a radio show called *The Seventeen Club* from a studio in O'Connell Street. Among other things, the show featured live music for teenage listening. The only snag early in 1963 was that the showbands who were involved had to play live on the show. Recording equipment was fairly primitive and bands weren't used to blowing into 'dead' mikes in a confined space where every bum note was picked up and kept for posterity. The standard of professionalism and musicianship had to be fairly good to sound any way presentable under these conditions. Gay Byrne, being a great pro himself, was very helpful and must have been pleased with our efforts because we were called back to do a second show a few weeks later.

With every month that passed we were gaining experience, going forward into new things, and after only two years on the road, we were offered the trip of a lifetime. We were going to America, New York, Boston, Chicago, San Francisco, Las Vegas, the sort of places I only heard of in songs and saw at the pictures. I remember thinking, at twenty years of age, if I was still working in a factory, the furthest I would get from Patrick Street would be to one of the 'An Óige' youth hostels close to Dublin, on my bike, with a haversack on my back. I was all excited about the trip and just couldn't wait to see the glitter, the fashions, Broadway, the skyscrapers, all the places I only dreamed about two years before. Commenting that New York could be extremely cold in November, our manager Tom splashed out on heavy sheepskin jackets for each member of the band, which were put to very good use during the tour. New uniforms featuring orange jackets were also bought to give an Irish flavour to the ensemble.

So, armed with our instruments, posters, hand-out photographs of the band in glossy colour in their thousands, changes of uniforms, wool jackets, beetle boots, a well-rehearsed arrangement of the 'Stars and Stripes', and in a blaze of publicity, we headed for the New World. Little did we know that Murphy's Law, not Pat's, would have a big say in this twelve-thousand-mile trip into the unknown.

The American nightmare

I wonder do they still play 'Danny Boy' over the PA system in the jets when they're landing in America after leaving the Emerald Isle. When this happened on the Boeing 707 touching down in New York on the start of our tour, I thought 'Why do they do that?' as I brushed a tear from my eye, feeling homesick already. As early as standing in the airport arrivals area, I was looking out for Clark Gable or Cary Grant, even Jerry Lewis would have done.

Although it was obvious that America was thirty years ahead of us in technology, everything else was very ordinary, there was no high fashion, the people looked and dressed the same as we did. As I walked about New York, I thought the atmosphere was cold, the weather was cold and the people were cold. I was disappointed to discover that all those Doris Day movies were just a pack of lies. I will have to admit that I fell in love with the selection of winter jackets in the clothes shops. They were fabulously designed and made, and very cheap, as was the amazing selection of childrenswear. The styles and designs of children's clothes were twenty-five years ahead of anything we had in Ireland. I went into the huge Maceys, clothes shop and as I was browsing around I asked one of the assistants where the ladies' slacks were on display. When she pointed to a rack nearby, I said, 'No, they are all men's slacks.' She contradicted me and repeated that they were for ladies. It was my first introduction to a zip in the front, rather than the usual side position, in girls' slacks. I bought two magnificent ski jackets, one in black and white, like the markings on a piebald pony, with thick black fur on the hood and sleeves, the other in turquoise with beige trimmings on the sleeves and hood. The jackets were twenty-two dollars each and they turned a few heads when I wore them at home in Ireland. What turned ladies' heads in America was the £2.19.11 navy suit that I had bought in C & As in London. One young woman was so impressed with its cape-top and check plaid collar with tight miniskirt underneath that she wanted to buy it from me. I refused to sell, of course, as it was far too cold to walk back to the hotel in my slip. I would gladly have sold her the three flashy dresses I bought in the French shop in Dublin before I came over, because I never got to wear them. I had thought that, being in America, I would be going to an occasional night club, like the Cocacabana, but it wasn't to be. There was nothing organised, we just seemed to drift around aimlessly, taking in this and that in casual gear. I never got to wear the dresses back home either, so they were certainly a bad buy.

Our week-long stay in the Woodward Hotel in the Big Apple was to haunt me for years afterwards. As always when I travelled with the band, I slept on my own and Jimmy shared a room with some of the boys. In America, this was to prove the most frightening experience of my life. As soon as we arrived in the hotel we found out that a murder had taken place there, causing as much reaction among the residents as the weather forecast. I couldn't sleep because my room was like an oven, with no way of controlling the heat. I had the window closed and a couple of scissors caught in the latches so no one could get in from the fire-escape outside. The tiles in the bathroom were so hot I had to stand on towels to wash myself, and I had to wait until I was actually going out to put my clothes on because I was constantly perspiring. The first night there, a man tried to force my door open. I could see part of his face through the small space the chain on the door allowed. I had the light on and was sitting up in bed, so he must have seen me as well. When he went away I literally trembled in my bed. As a direct result of this experience I couldn't sleep unless the light was on, right up to the time I got married.

Taking the lift down to the ground floor the next morning on my own was the first and the last time I stepped into a lift in America alone. Sealed into a confined space, I was confronted by three nasty-looking men, who without as much as a greeting tore me to pieces with their hateful eyes. After a couple of nights on my own, trying to sleep, jumping every time I heard a noise, and thinking my nerves would crack, I made my way, feeling frightened and lonely, to the big room that four of the band were sharing. When I explained my position, the boys just threw a mattress and blanket on the floor and said not to worry, I would be as safe as a house with them. And so I was. I had a sound sleep for the first time since landing in New York, with Paddy, Noel, Brendan and Jimmy as my guardian angels.

I laugh when I think of, not only having my hair roots brightened with Hiltone, a toothbrush and Jimmy's steady hand, but also videoed by Brendan. What could I do? American hairdressers had never seen, let alone tackled, a head like mine, so with the exception of a disastrous trip to a salon in Chicago, I did all the building on my beehive myself, and when the roots needed doing, it was back to the old reliable Hiltone and toothbrush. Thankfully, I had learned to manage my hair on my own while travelling around Ireland, so America didn't present any big problems that way. The naval uniform was a godsend because I didn't have to worry about what to wear on stage.

The biggest drawbacks of all were the exhausting car journeys across America and back. Yes, we travelled everywhere in a huge nine-door stationwagon. As we played our first weekend dances in New York, we were blissfully unaware of the chain of events that would see us journeying down endless highways, through countless toll-bridges, over mountains, across deserts, in heat and in cold and in vain. Although the dances in New York were enjoyable, I was surprised how badly lighted and smelly the ballroom was.

Happily, I can't say the same about Carnegie's Restaurant, where Bill Fuller, a charming man and the promoter of the tour, brought us for a meal. This famous eating house served me up a steak as big as one of my mother's apple cakes. Their speciality was a double or triple steak and trimmings sandwich, the likes of which I was told people travelled a long way to savour, and we had never seen in Ireland.

Another one of my rare enjoyable moments in New York was when we visited Birdland, the famous jazz club. Maynard Ferguson, a world-famous trumpet player, and his Big Band, supported by another jazz group, were playing there. I thought we'd have to queue to get in, even though we went at three in the afternoon. Apart from ourselves, there were only about three other people in the club. We sat there and were treated to a spectacular Big Band show. They blew up a storm, featuring some of the best musicians in the world. After seeing this performance we said we would never complain about playing in front of a small crowd again.

When we finally set out in our huge stationwagon to our first stop in Chicago, the first thing I noticed was how repetitive everything was. Highways leading to toll-bridges, then Howard Johnson or Horn and Hardart cafés, back to the highway, more toll-bridges, and still more of the same cafés. The food in the cafés was as monotonous as the highways and toll-bridges. The same menus, the same taste, they even looked the same, but they were a welcome sight, if only to stretch our legs and freshen up after hours of travelling. Our driver, an Irish-American named Gene Quinn, whom the boys called 'Tunney', was more robot than man, and I'm convinced he must have suffered from insomnia. It was no trouble for him to be behind the wheel for over thirty-six hours with only a couple of thirty-minute stops for food, and he drove as if the world had caught fire and he had to catch the last spaceship leaving from the other side of America. The stationwagon actually did catch fire and he was reluctant to stop to put it out. We eventually pulled over and the flames were extinguished with snow from the side of the road. The journeys were so long that I recall Jimmy saying to me that he shaved, grew a beard, and shaved again, without leaving the limo. The people in the mid-west of America, down-to-earth country people, were very friendly. They always made us feel welcome when we stopped to eat or buy a souvenir and it was always 'Y'all come back now' when we were leaving.

The windy city lived up to its name, and it was cold too, as we arrived in Chicago prior to our ill-fated trip out west. The dances were uneventful and the only couple of things that stick out in my mind about Chicago were both embarrassing. The one and only time I tried to have my hair done in America, in a salon, was in Chicago. We were staying just outside the city centre, in a motel, and when I learned that there was a ladies' hairdressers less than a mile away I decided to walk there without telling anyone. As I walked up the road I should have 'copped on', there wasn't a soul in sight, no children playing outside their houses, nobody walking anywhere except 'little green Eileen from Ireland'. Men driving by hooted their car horns at me, others made remarks through open car windows, and a couple of cars pulled over to enquire about my 'well being'. I was lucky not to have been bundled into a car and never heard of since. Pat Murphy never cursed, the worst thing he ever called me was a 'loola', but even Pat would have found a few slightly soiled adjectives to describe this stupid female strolling along a lonely Chicago road on her own. The hairdresser hadn't a clue what I was talking about when I described back-combing and climbing curls, so I just settled for what she could do and started walking back along the same road again.

The other awkward moment was when I was asked to sing for a local radio station — live from the ballroom. They wanted an Irish song for their mainly Celtic listeners, so I wound up on the balcony of the ballroom, accompanied only by Pat Murphy on harmonica, singing 'Danny Boy' into a microphone attached to some machine or other. Pat sounded fine, but I could imagine my voice coming over the radio like someone singing down a phone-line with a peg on their nose.

The lights of Las Vegas were a welcome sight after climbing into the cold of the mountains, descending into the heat of the desert, and being shaken out of an uneasy sleep by the sudden noise of the car wheels rattling over warning grids approaching every toll-bridge. The flashy motel with twenty-four-hour TV and Las Vegas with twenty-four-hour gambling was the last thing I needed as I staggered out of our nine-door coffin and tried to get the blood circulating strongly enough in my legs to carry me to a bed. Las Vegas without lights would be like a birthday cake without candles, and if gambling stopped, people wouldn't know what to do with their coins. Even old ladies sat with bags of coins in front of them and spent hours pulling the handles, and I'd say some of the old dears after flushing the toilet would check to see if they had won anything. Las Vegas was only a short stopover before we travelled on to open a new ballroom in San Francisco on Saturday, 23 November 1963.

This gig was a real biggy, the grand opening of the luxurious Carousel Ballroom on Market Street, featuring ourselves, described as Europe's great dance attraction direct from Ireland, and Bobby Vinton from Hollywood, who had smash hits with 'Roses are Red' and 'Blue Velvet', plus our own Eileen Donaghy, a great Irish ballad singer. On Friday 22 November, before we set off for San Francisco, I was sitting on a swing in the grounds of the motel when I heard a woman screaming. She was running towards the motel shouting and crying 'He's been shot'. Being in America, I wasn't totally shocked at hearing that someone had been shot, so I just stood up and wondered was it her husband or son or brother she was screaming about. Some of the boys in the band came out of the motel and asked what was wrong. The woman blurted out through her tears that President Kennedy had been shot. Did you ever feel that this was it, nothing else could happen, and then it did. Up until now, I wasn't really enjoying the trip, it wasn't what I expected, but I was resigned to see it through, and then this happened. I didn't know what to think. I was sorry, shocked, confused and afraid, all at the same time. The boys were throwing all sorts of ideas and questions about — he might only be wounded! Listen to the radio! I hope he's all right! Who's in charge now? Is the country safe if he dies? What's the point in driving to San Francisco? What'll we do if all the gigs are cancelled? 'Tunney', our driver, had no doubts about where he was going, to Hell or to San Francisco, he had a job to do, no he had a destiny, to drive like mad all over America until his contract was fulfilled. As the ninth door was slammed shut and the radio switched on, we sat silently listening to the news bulletins, gradually becoming more concerned for the president than any journeys or gigs. About an hour into our journey it was announced that President Kennedy was dead. Nobody commented, just silence, and I cried. When we pulled into a garage for our usual 'High Test' gasoline, there was an eerie tension in the air. The people were sorrowful, they were angry, and they were frightened — it was a bad time to be in America.

The journey back across the width of America was even worse than the one out, with tension and uncertainty everywhere. There was nothing on television or in the newspapers except the reliving of the final moments in the life of the president. Everywhere we stopped, the conversation was the same — who killed him and for what reason? It seemed that everything people were doing over these fateful days was put on the back boiler, including our so-called tour of America. I began to really long to be home again.

Boston was the last place we were to play before we left the States, and since the few days of mourning for the president had passed, the gig went ahead. After the dance in Boston, the band stayed back and had a few drinks in a party atmosphere. I don't know whether we were celebrating the 'success' of the tour, drowning our sorrows, or thankfully toasting our departure from the Land of the Free. As the final couple of drinks were being consumed, Jimmy and I went out to sit in the nine-door limo outside the ballroom. Being late November, it was a bitterly cold night and we were well clad as we sat waiting for the rest of the lads. We were sitting in the third seat back from the driver's, and when the door in front of us opened we thought it was one of the band getting in. The door closed and a male voice said 'Let's go'. We didn't recognise the voice or the person in front of us. What we did notice was that he didn't have any shirt or vest on, in fact he was totally naked. It didn't matter to me, naked or fully clothed, there was a stranger in the car, so I jumped out and put distance between us. Just then, some of the boys came out of the ballroom and saw the funny side of the situation — there was no danger here, the poor fellow certainly wasn't going to pull a gun on anybody.

The man was coaxed out of the car and somebody suggested getting a taxi to take him home. He wasn't drunk, dispelling the notion that he had come from one hell of a party, and yet we couldn't make out what he was saying, or doing, in the middle of a bitterly cold night, in his nude. A taxi was 'flagged' down, and when the Afro-American driver was asked to take our friend in his birthday suit home, he simply shook his head and said, 'Are you kiddin', Man! He ain't got no pockets', and drove away. The last I saw of our freezing streaker was his by now blue bottom moving in tandem with Tunney, our kamikaze driver, down the street in search of a policeman who would bring the whole episode to some sort of conclusion.

Back in New York, I got extremely anxious to be home and just couldn't wait for our scheduled flight in about forty-eight hours. There was an earlier flight, but it went directly to London, so I would have had to get another flight from there to Dublin. I actually wanted to do this, but was talked out of it while we all waited patiently counting the hours.

Eileen

Touching down at Shannon prolonged the agony of a long transatlantic flight, but when we finally left the aircraft in Dublin, I felt like kissing the ground. Just as many members of our families that saw us off a month earlier came to welcome us home. The amount of kissing and hugging wouldn't have been greater if we had just been released after years as hostages in a Beirut prison. The sight of a roaring fire and the smell of freshly baked apple tart brought tears to my eyes as I walked into our flat. Kicking off my shoes and throwing myself down in an armchair, I thought, 'Home again, this is Heaven.'

1. Eileen's paternal grandparents, Charles and Catherine Reid, c 1880.

2. Eileen's maternal grandmother,
Bridget Delaney.

3. Eileen's parents, Charlie and Eileen, with their first-born, Noel.

4. Eileen's father, Charlie Reid, capped for Ireland in 1931. Ireland drew 1–1 against Spain in Barcelona.

5. Eileen with younger sister Beatrice (left) and brother Robert, 1948.

6. *The Iveagh Buildings, west front, looking out onto Patrick Street, where Eileen was born. The window of Reid's flat is the fifth from the left, on the top floor.*

7. *The Iveagh Play Centre, affectionately known as the 'Bayno', where Eileen spent many happy childhood hours.*

8. *Eileen on O'Connell Bridge, First Communion day, 1950.*

9. *Eileen (left) with her sister Beatrice in St Patrick's Park, 1953.*
The Iveagh Play Centre may be seen in the background.

10. *Beatrice Gaskins, better known as Auntie Beattie.*

11. Eileen (back right) takes part in the school concert, held in the back yard of St Bridget's Holy Faith School, Clarendon Street, 1950.

12. St Bridget's Holy Faith School, Clarendon Street, c 1950. Eileen was a student here from 1947 to 1957.

13. Eileen's parents, Charlie and Eileen, crossing O'Connell Bridge, c 1945.

14. Eileen's older sister Kitty at her first dress dance. (Left to right, front) Kitty, Eileen's mother, and family friend Marie O'Connor. (Left to right, back) Gerry O'Connor (Kitty's future husband), with Eileen's brothers Noel and Charlie.

15. The Reid family celebrate Charlie Junior's birthday.
(Left to right, seated) Kitty, Noel, Patrick, Eileen, Mam, Dad, Charlie.
(Standing) Beatrice, Robert.

16. Eileen's mother made her own social life at home.
Pictured at one of her sing-songs are (from left) Mr Brocklebank, Eileen's
mother, Mrs Brocklebank, Mrs and Mr Rowantree.

17. The Jacob's Ladies' Football Team, 1960 (Eileen is second from left, back row). It was at the Jacob's dance, where Eileen sang a few songs with the band, that she was spotted and invited to audition for a new band, the Cadets.

18. Eileen in her Cadets' uniform.
The beehive hairstyle became her trademark.

19. The Cadets, 1963. Eileen, Pat Murphy, Brendan O'Connell, Gerry Hayes, Jas Fagan, Jimmy Day, Willie Devey, Noel McGann, Paddy Burns.

20. Eileen's future husband, Jimmy Day, nicknamed 'The Vicar' by the other Cadets, 1962.

21. The Cadets, 1963.
Eileen's feet were practically deformed from squeezing her toes into the 'fashionable'
pointed shoes seen here.
(Back, left to right) Noel McGann, Gerry Hayes, Pat Murphy, Paddy Burns, Brendan
O'Connell, Jas Fagan. (Front, left to right) Willie Devey and Jimmy Day.

22. (Left to right) Tom Costelloe (Cadets' manager), Eileen, Roy Orbison and Jimmy Day, 1963.

23. On the set of Thank Your Lucky Stars, July 1963. (Left to right) Mick Jagger, Pete Murray and Brian Jones of the Rolling Stones, Helen Shapiro, Pat Murphy, Eileen, and other newcomers to the pop music scene.

24. *The Cadets meet the Beatles at the Gresham Hotel, Dublin, November 1963. (Left to right) Tom Costelloe (Cadets' manager), Jimmy Day, Jas Fagan, Paul McCartney, Eileen, John Lennon, Brendan O'Connell, Pat Murphy and Noel McGann.*

'Wedding Dress'

*1*964 and 1965 were possibly the Cadets' best years in terms of recording, and during this time we were probably at the height of our popularity. Very early in 1964 we began a thirteen-week sponsored programme on Radio Luxembourg. Every Wednesday for a quarter of an hour the station's listeners were treated to the best of the Cadets by courtesy of Marlow Cleaners. Radio Éireann got in on the act and booked us for twenty-six weeks every Thursday afternoon at 2.30 pm. All these fifteen-minute sessions had to be pre-recorded and the band was so busy that we recorded them on our night off or any other time we could squeeze in. If we were going to Donegal or Kerry and we were meeting early, we could listen in at 2.30 pm and hear 'Carnival time with the Cadets', which we always began with our signature tune 'Anchors Away' in Dixieland jazz style. We were getting plenty of air time, but all the songs we played were other people's hits, and although we were satisfied with the business we were doing, a hit record was a must for us if we were to keep up with the competition. We had recorded material before that had been given to us by people outside the band and we were to do it again later, but ironically, all the major hits we had came from our own tried and trusted method. Brendan, our guitarist, had probably the best collection of country music in Ireland at the time, and we would simply sit down and listen to dozens of potentially recordable songs, and then have a vote on what we thought was the best option. An old Jim Reeves song called 'Fallen Star' was chosen in this way and was recorded in Pinewood Studios in Bray, just outside Dublin. It was released in May 1964 and took off instantly. I remember listening to Larry Gogan's radio show *Top Ten* at around one o'clock on a Thursday afternoon. When he announced that the Number One song in the Irish hit parade was 'Fallen Star' by Eileen Reid and the Cadets, I turned to my mam and said, 'I don't feel any different', to which she replied, 'That's good, stay that way.'

I don't know who started the idea of buying a certain amount of your own records to boost sales and help a song's ratings in the charts, but like flashy posters, coloured handouts, and bigger, more luxurious coaches, once it started you had to keep up with the rest. Even the genuine popular hits had to be helped along, and with the very notable exception of our monster hit 'I Gave My Wedding Dress Away', we did a little bit of buying ourselves. Discs were 7/6, or $37\frac{1}{2}$ pence in today's money, and I had a good laugh one night after a gig somewhere in Mayo when Pat, in a small tea-room, gave each of us £2.2.6 to buy three records apiece. One of the tea ladies saw me receiving the money, and when Pat left the room she came to me and very sympathetically said, 'I know it's none of my business but I think you deserve more than that.' Of course we wouldn't go into a record shop and buy one of our own recordings, so we just asked a family member to spend the £2.2.6 in three different shops. The myth, that dumping truckloads of showband records was the cause of most of the pollution in our rivers, is definitely not true.

With the success of 'Fallen Star', the Cadets were the first showband featuring a girl singer to get into the Irish 'Top Ten'. I was the first Irish female singer to have a Number One hit in the Irish charts and the song itself had the distinction of being the first top hit actually recorded in Ireland. Even though I had appeared on television a few times in England and Ireland, it was always with the band and as part of a larger group, dividing the camera nine ways, so to speak. But claiming undivided attention, head and shoulders, side profile, full frontal and facial from one of these cruel, uncompromising machines, was to be a different ballgame altogether. I'll never forget the first time this happened to me. I was a guest on the panel of Larry Gogan's *Pickin' the Pops* show on RTE and was in great form, talking a mile a minute and giving my opinions on the music he was playing with great enthusiasm. The programme was recorded in the early afternoon, and after really enjoying myself, I got the bus home quickly to see the show at tea-time. When I saw myself on our black and white TV, I left the room in tears. Half of Ireland saw me dressed in a cream suit, with practically no make-up or lipstick, and a pile of blonde hair stacked a foot high on my head. I came over like a white blob. I was like Marge Simpson with a bag of flour thrown over her. And it didn't stop there. The side-angle shots had me looking like the Wicked Witch of the West, all nose and chin. I hated it when Mam consolingly patronised me with 'Don't be upset, you were lovely'. I was a little self-conscious after that and took Pat Murphy's advice to at least wear a little more lipstick.

Perhaps the reason I got on so well with the girls who clamoured around the stage was that I held no threat for them with regard to the attentions of the band members. I may not have been beautiful, but I had a look of my own with my flashy uniform and blonde beehive. I began to notice that blonde girls were copying my hairstyle, so I must have had some redeeming features. After 'Fallen Star' had enjoyed eight weeks in the charts, we decided on a follow-up recording. We went back to Brendan O'Connell's country music 'supermarket' again and narrowed our choice to two possibilities — a catchy Dixiecups number called 'Chapel of Love' and a real weepy Kitty Wells song entitled 'I Gave My Wedding Dress Away'. At one stage, because 'Wedding Dress' had a speaking part in the middle, it was thought that it might not be suitable for the dancing public, and maybe 'Chapel of Love' would be a better choice, but the unusual title and haunty melody of the Kitty Wells classic won out and brought about the biggest hit the Cadets ever had.

Most of the top showbands used to put the 'show' into the band by doing comedy numbers, dressing up and getting the crowd to stand and watch. We were no exception, and this led to the idea of me wearing a wedding dress on stage. At the time we were doing comedy sketches like the 'school around the corner', with two of the boys dressing up as schoolkids and being asked questions by me playing the part of Patsy Crosby, and getting hilarious answers à la Brendan Grace and Bottler style. On other occasions I pranced around in a pair of pyjamas during 'James Hold the Ladder Steady', and Willie, our drummer, went into convulsions doing the 'Laughing Policeman'. There wasn't a dry eye in the ballroom as Jimmy performed the sad tale of 'Little Rosa', and we even had a barking arrangement of 'There's No Place Like Home', with four of the lads imitating howling dogs.

'You wouldn't, would you?' Pat asked in surprise when I told him, on the way home from a gig, that I would wear a real wedding dress on stage when the record was released. The dancing public by now were used to seeing the top bands doing all in their power to be different, and this was what the business was all about, standing out from the rest. The idea of wearing the dress on stage was put into motion as I walked into the French shop in Wicklow Street in Dublin and paid thirty-three pounds, from band funds of course, for an absolutely beautiful wedding dress. The maker of the dress could never have dreamed that it would be worn over three hundred times, without being repaired or even cleaned. I wore it till if fell off me, metaphorically speaking of course.

The song was a monster hit for the band and the whole idea surrounding it was a publicity manager's dream, taking in the great visual effect for television and stage. The first time I wore the wedding dress on stage in Dublin was in the New Arcadia Ballroom in Bray, and there must have been three thousand people at the dance. I had to sing our hit several times to dancers crammed around the stage like sardines in a tin. We toured all around the country, with the dress the centre of attraction, even in the dreaded marquees. Showbands could write volumes about their experiences in marquees, where they divided their time between balancing on one leg in the mucky grass behind the stage, while putting the other into the trouser leg of the band suit, trying not to be electrocuted, and looking for a toilet. I don't have to tell you what it was like, getting onto a makeshift stage, surrounded by mud, on a rainy night, in a wedding dress. My worst experience with regard to looking for a loo was when one night after a gig we went back to a house nearby for a cup of tea. We were in a country area about a hundred miles from Dublin, so after drinking orange on stage and tea afterwards I enquired from the woman of the house if I could use the toilet. Her young daughter was given the task of showing me where the loo was, so I followed her. I wound up outside the house, in some kind of shed with straw on the ground. The girl told me I could 'go' there, and left me in pitch darkness. 'To go or not to go', that was the question, and the answer came in the sound of a pig grunting, or maybe it was a hoarse cow. I didn't wait to find out, and ten seconds later I was through the back door and into the house again. I faced a two-and-a-half-hour journey literally holding my own, and when I got home I thought I would burst before I got to the top floor of the flats.

It was later decided to raffle the wedding dress over a period of months, selling tickets in every ballroom, with the proceeds going to the Central Remedial Clinic. Apart from coming to see the band and the dress, dancers were coming to buy raffle tickets, so we really got mileage out of the whole 'wedding dress' thing. I wore the dress six nights a week while performing the song, for about a year, and from trailing along the floors of hundreds of ballroom stages, the bottom part got so torn, tatty and dirty that I was embarrassed wearing it. Girls would come around the stage and feel the dress, probably thinking 'nice material, pity about the state of it'. When the draw for the dress, or rather, one exactly like it, took place in Dublin, a man from Letterkenny in County Donegal won, and when we played in Letterkenny he stepped up to claim his prize. He didn't even buy a ticket, he was given one, and being married with three sons, wasn't interested in the dress. Pat offered him the thirty-three pounds we paid for it, but he refused this, saying the dress was worth far more than that. I left them to work it out and they must have come to some agreement, because I don't remember taking my wedding dress to court.

It's funny, when you're successful in showbusiness, how the general public think that your whole life is glamorous and different twenty-four hours a day. In reality the only exciting parts are the hours spent on stage; the rest of the time is as humdrum as the life of any worker. I remember a reporter from a magazine called the *New Spotlight* asked me about the eight men in my life, referring to the boys in the Cadets. The boys were there at the time and when it came to the question of hobbies or sports they discovered that they were unfit and had no hobbies to speak of. Nobody played any kind of sport, except maybe Brendan, who sometimes played golf at six o'clock in the morning. Darts and poker were ruled out as physical sports, so I tried desperately to think of something interesting to say about each of them. Pat's genuine hobby was collecting lead soldiers and painting them in regimental uniforms, and he still has an award-winning display of them today. As for the rest of the band, here is what we came up with concerning what they did off-stage. I said Jimmy was a hard worker, which was very interesting, and Paddy took his music seriously and we called him 'Flossie'. Don't go away, there's more! Willie's ambition was to own his own harem, Noel wanted to earn enough money to retire as soon as possible, and poor Jas Fagan, who liked an occasional flutter on a horse, was credited with wanting to own his own gambling casino. Brendan was described as being tuned in to Chet Atkins, so much so that it was difficult to get onto his wavelength at all. We were absolutely stumped when it came to what to say about Gerry Hayes, our keyboard player, whom we called 'Gounod'. To wind up the reporter's assignment we boldly told him that Gerry collected clocks. I told him that 'Gerry eats, sleeps and thinks clocks', and as my nose grew longer I said he had all sorts, shapes and sizes of clocks, and wanted Big Ben on his mantelpiece. The strange thing is that people would be inclined to believe nonsense that was written just to fill up a magazine article, but find real truth harder to swallow. No one would believe that the band made a fourteen-track LP in less than two days in London, and the only stimulants we used to give us strength were Mars bars and milk. The LP was simply entitled 'The Cadets' and was the first Pye Golden Guinea LP by an Irish showband. It created a sales record in Ireland, and we received a Golden Guinea Award from Mr John Woods of Pye Records. The LP was described as a capsule version of our stage act and featured all the vocal and instrumental talents we had.

When we recorded 'Are You Teasin' Me' as a follow-up to 'Wedding Dress', it was decided to put brass and a real 'punchy' beat into this old Ira and Charlie Louvain song. It was thought that this sort of sound would have a better chance of making it internationally. It was a hit here all right, but it didn't make an impression across the water. Phil Coulter, who later wrote Eurovision winner 'Puppet on a String', and an English songwriter called Tommy Scott, were working closely with us trying to find the right format for a British hit. We did actually enter the British charts for one week with a song called 'Jealous Heart' in June 1965, but that's where it ended. The B side of the same disc, 'Right or Wrong', did well for us in Ireland, but an international hit eluded us. I suppose our LP told us where we stood; we were neither country, beat, pop nor jazz, we were a combination of everything, in fact we were an Irish showband and would never be anything else.

We had one more go in London, recording an EP with

four songs, featuring myself and Jimmy, and a single with me on one side and Jimmy on the other. The single featured an old favourite 'Baby Roo', which brought back a few memories. Phil Coulter and Tommy Scott helped tremendously with these recordings and they were very optimistic about showbands making a big impact in Britain. I remember when we were recording 'Are You Teasin' Me' in London, we brought our equipment into what we thought were the studios, until a very startled porter told us that we were in a Methodist conference hall and the recording studio was next door. Maybe if we had recorded in a church we might have had a bit more luck in the English charts.

I can make you a star

Ajournalist asked me recently if I would love to have
made it really big in the sixties. I said I could have
and he asked me to explain. I told him, but he
never printed the story. Perhaps it was because I
couldn't name names as it were. Still not naming people for
obvious reasons, I will explain how, not only I, but Jimmy
too, could have been big stars in England.

The Cadets' powerful representatives in England thought
it very possible that the band could be marketed there, and
so they set the wheels in motion. I don't know all the details
about what was planned for us, but Tom, our manager,
wanted to give us every chance to go further and he backed
the idea.

Part of the game plan was a prestigious appearance in the
Lyceum Ballroom in London and a lavish champagne
reception for the heads of the music trade in the plush
offices of our reps in England. When we arrived as special
guests we found ourselves ankle-deep in carpets, sipping
champagne — in my case it was orange — and rubbing
shoulders with the *crème de la crème* of recording companies
and practically every star in the top half of the British charts,
including the guest of honour, who had a Number Four hit
at that time. We were dressed in our blue and white naval
uniforms, with me sporting a big flower in front of my
elevated hairstyle to hide my dark roots. The whole
glamorous scene just oozed with success and well-being.
Everyone seemed to have made it big in this exclusively rich
mutual admiration society. While we were trying to socialise
with these VIPs, Jimmy and I were discreetly asked into the

private office of the head of this very powerful agency. Although we didn't know for what reason, we found ourselves in this holy of holies, and wondered what we were going to hear as the door was closed behind us.

There were two people in the room, the boss himself and a lady who turned out to be his wife. As, on his invitation, we sat down and made ourselves comfortable, he didn't sit in the chair behind the big desk, but rather on the side of the desk. I thought this was to create a relaxed, informal atmosphere as he began speaking to us. His wife sat a distance away just listening attentively. Without beating about the bush he started telling us the facts of life about the whole music business. He took us totally by surprise when he said he was not interested in the entire Cadets showband, just myself and Jimmy. We let him carry on talking, and boy did we learn a lot in the next few minutes. He said, 'You've heard of Paul and Paula?' We said we had. 'Well,' he announced, 'I want you to be Britain's answer to them.' This American duo were making big waves on the pop scene in the United States at the time. He told us that if we thought we could make it into the British charts by touring around with the Cadets, we were wasting our time. No matter how popular we became or what records we made, we would never crash the charts on our own, it just would not work. He then pointed out a young girl who was at the reception and I knew of her because we were doing her hit record in the band. Next, he brought me over to the window of his office and showed me a beautiful silver Rolls Royce parked outside. 'That', he said, 'belongs to the father of the girl I pointed out, and as you know she occupies the Number Four slot in the charts. This man bought a top position in the British charts for his daughter for her eighteenth birthday.' Seemingly, the owner of the Rolls Royce came to the right man. The big boss wasn't finished yet, and he continued to demonstrate his influential power. As we looked out onto one of London's busy streets, he said he could pick, at random, any young man walking along, put a guitar around his neck and make him a star. He was very keen to prize us away from the band, and he directed most of his attention on me, probably of the opinion that a girl would be more prone to accepting the glitter of star status. The bottom line was that if we left the Cadets and worked for him, he could make us big stars in Britain and Ireland overnight.

Without hesitating, we both said no, we would rather stay with the Cadets. He probably thought we were both mad, there wouldn't be a youngster in any part of the world, struggling in the music business, that wouldn't have jumped at this opportunity. We were not stupid or naïve, and although we didn't know the power that a special few had over the entire pop industry, we did know that we wouldn't be given this stardom as a gift, there would be a heavy price to pay. Living out of suitcases, travelling all over Britain and beyond, away from Ireland and home indefinitely, gruelling schedules under a two- or three-year contract, and all this for a weekly wage of certainly not more than we were getting in the Cadets. We would be stars waiting to fade, milked dry while shining, and discarded when the bubble burst, to try to carry on living a former glory. There were artists who survived this trial by fire and struggled around the English clubs for years afterwards making a living, while hundreds more gave up after their short taste of stardom and were never heard of again, and then there were the élite handful who were lucky enough to be kept in the big time for many many years.

Jimmy and I enjoyed being in the Cadets, we liked the company of the boys in the band and loved being at home. There was something wrong with the set-up we had been listening to, and as the boss of this big agency smiled at our rejection of his offer, we left his office, viewing the superstars at the reception in a very different light.

From constantly styling my own hair I became interested in hairdressing and decided to open a small salon in Aungier Street on the southside of Dublin, about fifteen minutes' walk from where I lived. My sister's husband Gerry O'Connor introduced me to a friend of his who owned a salon, with a view to getting me some advice. The only advice he gave me was, 'Don't go into the hairdressing business.' It was sound advice that fell on deaf ears because, seeing that his salon was situated not too far from my proposed one, I thought that he was just trying to discourage the pending competition. I was to regret not listening to this wise man, as my venture into the business was to turn out ten times worse than the American nightmare.

The salon was situated over a café in a brand new building, and everything I bought was brand new as well, all paid for in cash. I leased the premises and hired two first-class stylists, Marian and Eugene, who came to me from top hairdressing salons and brought most of their clients with them. Dickie Rock opened the salon in a blaze of publicity and things looked very healthy from the outset. My brother Robert was in charge of the business and did a wonderful job. He was a great public relations man with a winning personality, who got on very well with the staff. Oddly enough, my famous beehive hairstyle was to be the first financial thorn in my side because a lot of young girls were coming in and asking for the Eileen Reid look. The old wash, cut and blow dry was the bread and butter of most salons, but the style they were looking for in my salon took far more effort and time that it was worth. After a while I was singing in the band to subsidise the salon. The heavy overheads of lease, stock, electricity, wages, insurance, etc, were eating up everything I was earning in the band.

Although I was voted Number One female vocalist in Ireland four years in a row, it was decided to add to our vocal strength by signing a male singer. We did have excellent singers in the band, but they were instrumentalists as well, and none was fronting the band in the roll of a lead vocalist. Paul Green, a twenty-two-year-old Dubliner who had experience working the entertainment circuit in England, was signed up. We didn't christen him 'Onions', but that was the nickname he carried into the band. He was a wonderful singer, in the Sammy Davis mould, a gifted mimic and a natural comedian. Paul arrived as we took possession of a new luxury coach which had every amenity except a bar and toilet. We were really travelling in style, with a built-in stereo system which we used for rehearsing new songs, a heated wardrobe, reclining aircraft seats, overhead racks, and plenty of room for walking up and down. Nobody slept while Onions was on board, he just talked all the time, telling stories about his escapades in London and reeling off jokes, all clean, by the dozen. We put down the backing track of a song called 'If I had My Life to Live Over' in Eamonn Andrews' Studios in Dublin, with the help of a Noel Kelehan arrangement, for Paul's first record with the band, but Paul was never to feature on it. Things just didn't work out and Paul's destiny was not to include displaying his many talents with the Cadets. On leaving the band he returned to England to continue his career there, and I do hope he found success and happiness over the years.

A lead male vocalist was still sought and Pat Murphy's eagle eye picked a real find in the shape of a twenty-year-old lad from Sion Mills, near Strabane in Northern Ireland. Gregory Donaghy had an infectious personality and a tenor voice second to none. His happy-go-lucky, boy-next-door image was a winner with the girls, and everyone in the band took to him straight away. As one big happy family we once again raided Brendan's nest of country golden eggs and came up with a huge hit called 'More than Yesterday', which took Gregory into the Irish charts and gave the Cadets a new lease of life. Gregory was always the life and soul of the party, and his laugh could be heard three blocks away. If we were rehearsing a song in the coach, we made sure Gregory wouldn't give it his all in case he'd smash the windscreen with a top C. That old Bing Crosby/Grace Kelly favourite 'True Love' was given the treatment by myself and Gregory on disc, and it did pretty well for us. We also did some duets together in our stage act, 'Cinderella Rockafella' being one I particularly enjoyed.

Moving into 1967, some of the boys in the band had lost their single status. Our drummer Bill Devey married Lilly, the girl of his dreams, Brendan caved in to the charms of raven-haired Cecily, my namesake Eileen became Paddy's 'plates', and even before the lads bit the dust, Noel had married his childhood sweetheart June, and Jas 'Walk Tall' Fagan had a flutter and won the heart of Mary. It looked as if Jimmy and I were going to be the last ones in the band to get married, and if Jimmy was to have his wish it would be sooner rather than later. He had asked me to marry him but I didn't give him a definite answer because I couldn't. The girls around the stage weren't the only ones captivated by Gregory's boyish charms. He had a magnetic personality and when he showed an interest in me I became infatuated with him. Although we fancied one another, we never went out on a date together or showed any signs of our fondness for each other in the band, and Jimmy certainly didn't suspect anything. When the Cadets played in Sion Mills, where Gregory's family lived, I met his mother, who was extremely friendly and seemed to like me a lot. As this situation continued, I began to have doubts about my relationship with Jimmy. I still liked Jimmy and didn't want to hurt him, so I was really torn between the two of them. I was in an awkward situation, but felt that Gregory would make stronger advances if Jimmy was out of the equation. Gregory and Jimmy were good friends and I knew the whole affair was awkward for Gregory as well. I made up my mind and broke off my relationship with Jimmy. I hated doing it but I had to test this 'liking' I had for Gregory. When Jimmy and I parted, the situation didn't seem to change between myself and Gregory. We still didn't show openly that we were more than friends and didn't go on dates.

The usual place to go when we were off on a Monday night was the Television Club in Harcourt Street on Dublin's southside, where a top showband would play to capacity crowds. Gregory and I would sometimes meet there and he'd leave me home, and that's as deep as our relationship got. When the summer break came, I was surprised to learn that Jimmy and Gregory had gone to Majorca for their holidays. Finding myself alone without either of them, I made enquiries about which travel agent they used, and a week later I walked into the same hotel they were staying in. We spent the next week enjoying ourselves like a happy family, and as far as I was concerned, nothing was learned or proven by my visit. After the holiday, nothing really dramatic happened between myself and Gregory, we just went on being attracted to each other, but not really doing anything about it, neither of us wanting to make any real show of commitment to the other.

In November of 1967 Jimmy's father died, and shortly after this I went back to Jimmy. I was now sure he was right for me. It was I this time who asked could we get engaged at Christmas and get married in June 1968, and a very surprised Jimmy agreed. When this news was announced, Gregory made stronger advances towards me, but I rejected them, being positive now that Jimmy was the one for me. Even up to and during the last week I spent in the band, before I got married, Gregory kept asking me to marry him and insisted that I was making a mistake marrying Jimmy. My final words were, 'No, Gregory, you and I were never meant for each other.'

Wedding bells

I would love to have had a much bigger splash at my hens' party, but funds just didn't allow it. I was still on the financial ropes thanks to my ailing hairdressing salon, and after Jimmy had forked out for the wedding, our honeymoon, and a substantial deposit on our new four-bedroomed home in Raheny, he was almost as broke as I was. My philosophy on money was: 'you had it or you didn't', and managing it was never a subject for serious consideration. Money was for spending, there were lovely things out there to buy, so if you had the money, you should go ahead and buy them. When I had plenty of money I never thought that other people had money problems, even my own family. I wasn't generous, and yet I wasn't mean, I was just thoughtless and wrapped up in my own affairs. All my money was gone before I learned any lessons on what it was supposed to be all about.

My hens' party was limited to family, a few friends from the entertainment world and some loyal fans. It was a fairly modest buffet affair in the Montrose Hotel, but having said that, if I had ten times as much money to spend we probably would have had to sit down to a feast with twice as many people there. I remember a couple of really nice girls from Belfast, who had been fans of the Cadets for years, came down to Dublin to celebrate with me in the Montrose. A couple of months earlier when the band was playing a date in Belfast, these same two girls acted very oddly when I invited them to my wedding. I knew they would be delighted to come but they seemed to have a problem. They took me to one side after the dance and said they would love to come

120

but, they informed me shyly, almost apologetically, they were Protestants. 'Is that all?' I said, 'So what! You're invited and you're coming, and don't worry about being at the wedding ceremony, you'll be in good company, half the Catholics in the church won't know whether to stand up or sit down either.'

I thought I would get a really 'way out', different sort of wedding dress in London, but I just wasn't mad about anything I saw there. 'What about the French shop and one like *the* wedding dress?' someone suggested. Not on your life, I knew I would feel as if I was going to work instead of my wedding, and besides, fashions were changing and I wasn't really impressed with any of the dresses in Dublin either. In the end, I decided to have it made, and I paid twenty-five pounds a yard for some beautiful material in Cassidys of Grafton Street. I fell in love with this magnificent white ribbon lace and left the sewing in the very capable hands of Cecily Watson, wife of our guitarist Brendan, who was a wonderful dressmaker. Cecily did a great job on my empire-line dress, which had a long trail, boat-shaped neck, sleeves to the elbows, a three-inch band of pearls under the bust and an inch-band on the arms. The back of the dress was so lovely that Cecily advised against a long veil. I bought the head gear, which consisted of a plain satin bow with beads and shoulder-length veil, in London. Cecily also made the bridesmaids' dresses, the material for which was bought in The Spinning Mill, Royal Avenue, Belfast. They had a very floral, short-sleeved, summery look, with a mixture of lime green, lavender and pink, which contrasted nicely with the tans of my sisters Kitty and Beatrice, and Jimmy's sister Helen. Jimmy's brothers, Kevin and Brendan, and my brother Robert, made up the rest of our closest helpers on the big day.

In our flat on the morning of the wedding, I was standing around for ages in my dress trying to get out of everybody's way. There was no big fuss made of me — everyone was totally occupied with their own appearance or with having a 'jar'. I certainly didn't feel like I was the centre of all the excitement.

When we got to the Church of St Nicholas of Myra, the grounds and the street outside were packed with people from all around the area. As I walked up the isle with my father, I could sense that he was moved by the whole wonderful atmosphere. When Jimmy and I came out of the church, there were so many people crowding the grounds that we couldn't get near the main wedding limousine. We quickly jumped into the second one, and with the help of the gardaí, drove slowly down a crowded Francis Street. When we got near the bottom of the street the driver stopped our car in the middle of the traffic, while we jumped out and got into the limo with all the ribbons on it. I must have shaken hands with half of the Liberties, because when I got time to take stock of myself as we drove to the hotel, I noticed that my white gloves were already well worn.

There were no showbiz celebrities at the reception, it was strictly a family affair, with the band members and some close friends being the only non-relatives present. The Cadets even came with us on our honeymoon, to sunny Torremolinos in Spain. We went on an earlier flight and joined up with some of the boys and their wives later. It was just like summer holidays with the Cadets, except this time I was married and when the holiday was over I wouldn't be going back on the road. I didn't mind this in the least because I was now in a different frame of mind. Marriage to me meant, first of all, having children, and I just couldn't wait to know the experience of having one of my own. I would have been very disappointed if I hadn't become pregnant straight away, but as it happily turned out, I was not to be disappointed.

It was tough, exciting and comical starting off life in 109 Grange Park Estate, Raheny, Dublin 5, moving in with nothing but the bare necessities. I laughed when I said to Jimmy that I didn't even have a 'bottom drawer', and he replied, 'You're lucky to have a drawer.' I have fond memories now, I repeat 'now', of eating off an ironing board until we got a table for the kitchen. Linen and ironing boards must have been the 'in thing' in wedding presents then, instead of, for instance, bedroom curtains and kitchen tables. Although my mother lived ten miles away from me, she was more concerned about what my neighbours thought than I was. 'When are you taking "those things" off the bedroom windows and putting real curtains up?' she would ask. 'When the real ones are ready,' I'd answer. 'When will they be ready?' 'When I have the money.'

I never tried to live up to the 'Joneses'. If I did anything to the house, inside or out, it was just for my own satisfaction. In these early days, 'keeping' the house was far more of a consideration than doing it up. I thought that my presence in the hairdressing salon would improve things there, and was confident that business would pick up and it would start paying for itself. Being pregnant with Pamela didn't help because I was suffering badly with morning sickness, and apart from that I found it hard to adjust to getting up in the morning after my nocturnal life in the band for so many years. I was eating myself stupid trying to ease the heartburn that was accompanying my morning sickness, and this indulging sent my weight up to over twelve stones. After looking at pieces of paper, morning, noon and night, that kept telling me, no, roaring at me, that this was overdue, that was needed and the other was running low, as well as haunting me with a constant merry-go-round of stamps, tax, rates, rent, wages, stock and staff problems, I finally came to a decision. I walked into the salon one day and told everyone that they were on two weeks' notice. I then sold everything in the shop at a huge loss and walked away from it. I didn't care or even realise that I would have to pay the remaining lease on the salon, which was another small fortune. I was skint, and even what Jimmy was bringing home wasn't enough to pay off my considerable debts.

A ray of hope came in the form of a phone call from the office of my old manager, Tom Costelloe. Brian Mulloy, who worked with Tom managing bands, asked me if I would be interested in doing cabaret gigs. I didn't really know what he meant by cabaret, so he filled me in on what was happening on the pub scene. Being a non-drinker, I never went out to pubs and wasn't aware of the big music business building up there. Brian had shown me a light at the end of my collapsed financial tunnel, but at that moment I was as big as a horse, completely out of shape and looking forward to getting bigger in the months ahead. I was so used to being the first to do this or achieve that in the Cadets, that I could see, heading the entertainment column, 'Eileen Reid, first thirteen-stone mother-to-be to kick her legs up on the pub cabaret scene.' Still, I was always an optimist. I remember a favourite quote of Jimmys that went, 'You would attempt to drive a herd of cows into a phone box, close the door behind you, and then call America.'

When my mother invited me to join her and Mr and Mrs Larry Rowantree one Sunday night as they went to hear Val Tino in the Drake Inn, a cabaret lounge in Finglas on the northside of Dublin, I accepted the invitation out of curiosity. I was only getting comfortable in my seat when the compère, a chap from Cork called Dale King, announced that a celebrity had walked in. I didn't mind that too much, but I nearly had a miscarriage when he added that I would be getting up to sing later. I wasn't dressed for the occasion, I wouldn't know what to sing, I was three months pregnant and there was no way I was budging from my seat, in fact I was frozen to my seat. Dale King kept calling my name when I refused to respond the first time, and had the huge crowd clapping expectantly. Although Dale and I became good friends and still are today, I could have strangled him then. When it became clear that I had no intention of singing, a few disgruntled customers close to me made remarks like 'Ah, don't mind her, she's too stuck up'. I felt dreadful, really embarrassed, and was glad to get out, vowing never to go back there again.

Pregnant or not, I took a gig, and my pub cabaret baptism

of fire began in Slatterys of Terenure, for which I was paid twenty-five pounds. Compère Pat O'Donnell introduced me on stage, while the band were handed nothing more than a list of the names of the songs I was going to sing. I just couldn't believe that cabaret was so different from fronting a danceband. I was suddenly confronted with all these people sitting down drinking beer and looking at me, almost defying me to entertain them. Fair play to the resident backing group, they just followed what I was singing to the best of their ability, which in this case was considerable. Jimmy used to do all the talking in the Cadets when we were on stage, and it never occurred to me that singing would not be enough if I was to be an entertainer. That night in Slatterys I sang one song after another, said goodnight and left the stage. When I got a return booking I improved my vocabulary, being really adventurous with such quips as 'My next song is called' or 'Is anyone celebrating a birthday?'. From adding a few words with each passing gig, I became quite good at it, and a few months later they couldn't shut me up. From these humble beginnings I learned how to project myself and develop as a performer, and I'm sure that I would never have progressed in theatre variety or acting roles had it not been for cabaret experience.

My liking for cabaret was growing, but not half as quickly as my figure, so I did what I could to conceal the obvious. I think I would have had Pamela during one of my performances but for the uncomplimentary remarks of the proprietor of an establishment where I was strutting my stuff with great gusto, at eight months into my pregnancy. I looked like Salomé in my handkerchief dress and thought no one would notice as I kicked my legs up and went through my routine with innocent abandon. It's a good job they didn't video the show or I think I would have retired after seeing it. I was blind to the way I looked and didn't see anything wrong with myself. After that laborious stint which was followed by the boss ticking off his manager about the necessities of hiring pregnant women to entertain his customers, I called a temporary halt to my newfound career and stayed at home to put my feet up. This was yet another lesson I was to learn: when you're a housewife, there's no such thing as putting your feet up. Despite dilemmas, disappointments and disasters, I was really happy and madly looking forward to having our first child, holding her in my arms, wondering what it would be like, and also what our future held in store, how we would tackle it, and would it be kind to us.

Part Three

Alone on the road

*I*swallowed hard when I was casually told, during one of my visits to the Coombe maternity hospital for a routine check-up, that some first-time mothers were in labour for up to eighteen hours. This was worse than doing six long gigs back-to-back without a break. The news didn't go down too well with me, but there was nothing I could do about it now. I needn't have worried, because everything was to run very smoothly from the time my waters broke while sitting with my mother in my former home. She got me to the Coombe Hospital in about five minutes and I was soon settled into a ward with five other 'patients'. About seven o'clock in the evening I got strong pains, which were repeated every five minutes. I'll never stick this for eighteen hours, I thought, so I called the nurse. I was hoping she wouldn't think I was a spoiled brat complaining about nothing. She just reassured me, saying I had a long way to go yet, and she left me waiting for the next stab of pain. Visitors started coming into the ward and one of them, seeing I was alone and in discomfort, offered to call the nurse for me. I took him up on his offer, and this time a couple of nurses pulled the screen around my bed and examined me. I was brought down to the delivery room, and at nine o'clock on 19 April 1969, Pamela was born. She was a big baby, weighing in at eight pounds thirteen ounces and leaving me needing stitches. Jimmy was with the Cadets playing a date in the north of Ireland and someone phoned the ballroom to tell him the good news. We were both delighted with our first child, who made a huge difference to our lives and brought us much closer together.

Coming into 1970, the Cadets were beginning to lose their popularity, with the musical emphasis now shifting to favour country and western bands and beat and ballad groups. Despite having a great country guitar and vocal sound, the Cadets were still mixing their programme and didn't really attack the country and western market. Pat Murphy was no longer travelling or playing with the band, and it soon became obvious that the Cadets were losing musical direction. Tom Costelloe was still the manager, and when business really started to drop, he offered some of its members a lifeline. At the time Tom was also managing a very successful folk singer named Johnny McEvoy, who up until then just backed himself on guitar. Putting a number of country/folk musicians behind Johnny with a view to touring the ballrooms seemed like a sound idea to Johnny and Tom. Brendan, Noel and Jimmy were offered positions in this new group, which Brendan and Noel accepted, and for many years they accompanied Johnny both here and abroad. Jimmy, however, didn't want to travel up and down the country any more, and decided to stay home and join some other members of both our families in the taxi business.

The Cadets had effectively broken up now, with the rest of the members going their separate ways. When trumpeter Paddy saw the crunch coming, he joined Tayto Ltd, and he still works for the great firm today, while continuing his involvement in music. Jas Fagan, who was originally a tailor by trade, built up a hugely successful men's outfitters in Thomas Street, Dublin. He still makes the stagewear for many of the top bands in Ireland, and he also made a complete set of uniforms for the Cadets when they made a short comeback in the late eighties. Willie and Gerry joined the cabaret circuit in Dublin, and Pat Murphy was soon back doing what he liked best, driving a band around Ireland. Gregory married Teresa shortly before the Cadets broke up, and afterwards went into cabaret, working north and south of the border before departing for Canada and ultimately the United States. He still fronts a band in America and comes home occasionally on holidays. After many years in the Johnny McEvoy band, Brendan joined the staff of St James's Hospital in south Dublin, while continuing to play guitar in various groups. Noel now owns a very successful garden centre on the Naas Road, and he still manages to 'thump out' the beat on his bass when the gigs come in.

I was glad to get back singing again after Pamela was born, but a lot of problems arose as I tried to do these dates on my own. I was beginning to get work in country parts, and these were to prove the most awkward gigs to do. Luckily I didn't get to do too many, because I could write a story about every one of them. I usually travelled alone by car and occasionally used the train and returned the next day. All my problems stemmed from the fact that I didn't have my own backing group with me — I simply couldn't afford to bring any musicians with the fees I was getting. I remember driving alone to some part of Kerry for fifty pounds, fighting tooth and nail to get the full fee, and driving back the same night. On another night when I met the band at the venue and showed them what songs I was doing, they enquired if I would sing them all in the same key — C. Depending on how many keys too high or too low the band were playing my songs, I screeched or belched my way through a very uncomfortable night's work. I always got requests to sing 'Wedding Dress', and very often this was to save the night for me when I was bogged down in the musical doldrums.

It is truly amazing what can turn a cabaret lounge full of long faces into a laughing and clapping competition. I was struggling to get any sort of attention one night in a packed country pub when this middle-aged man came in complete with brown battered cap, no teeth, wellies, and a big grin on his happy face. Although it was obvious that he was extremely well known, the rest of the audience kept a ring of confidence between themselves and him. He was very interested in what I was doing, in fact he was the only interested person there, and when he came up to the front of the band where I was performing, I started to include him in my act. Straight away, every person in the pub was watching the stage, some standing on chairs to get a better view. To the delight of the audience I asked him to sing along with me, and when we danced together we got even more tremendous applause than Patricia the Stripper. I dared him to kiss a woman sitting with friends near the bar, and the place went into an uproar. When the boss was paying me afterwards, he said I was wonderful, a really great act. I drove back home that night thinking that entertainment had come a long way.

In contrast, after a train journey to Cobh in County Cork, I had to get rid of someone during my cabaret act to save it from disaster. From the moment I arrived at this venue and before I took to the stage, the other members of the backing group, with the exception of the keyboard player, didn't want to know me or what I was performing. I thought I was the invisible woman as I tried to get their attention to run through my programme, but they just sipped their pints and ignored me. After asking as politely as I could without success, I gave up and finally sat down with the keyboard player, a friendly young man, and explained to him what I was doing.

When I at last hit the stage and started into my first song, it was evident that the drummer was not interested in the proceedings. He was just about keeping a beat and was talking with some friends in the audience at the same time. After a couple of songs, things got worse, and the pace of the show deteriorated into boredom. Then, would you believe, a drum solo, or rather the absence of it, saved the night. I came to a song called 'Da Doo Ron Ron', which starts with a drum roll. The drummer at this stage had got up my nose totally, and I just wasn't going to let him wreck the night. I moved back, stood beside the drums, and explained to the audience that I would count out one - two - three - four, and the drummer would rattle out on his snare-drum the introduction to the song. It was simple, I said. After I counted to four there was silence, no drum beat, he had dug his heels in and wouldn't play. I tried one more time, telling the packed singing lounge that every drummer in the country knew the little solo and it was as easy to play as falling off a stool. He didn't fall off the stool, but his negative response was just as effective, leaving me with no alternative but to say to the audience, 'We'll do it without the drums.' I asked everyone in the place to take out anything that would make a noise — loose change, jewellery, false teeth, even drumsticks if they had them — and beat out the rhythm on the tables in front of them after I counted to four. They responded perfectly, producing a loud, rattling solo, not only at the beginning, but right through the song, everywhere it was needed. The drummer just sat there, livid, and wouldn't get involved for the rest of the night. The people became my drummer from then on, and they enjoyed themselves so much that they gave me three encores. The keyboard player apologised to me afterwards for what happened, and in thanking him for his cooperation I explained that I didn't enjoy doing what I did with regard to our drummer friend, and happily I never had to do anything like that again.

Exchanging stories with fellow artists about experiences on stage was always great fun and the resident bands in lounges could match us with their own hilarious take-outs. A friend of mine called Eithne Dunne, known in cabaret circles as 'the blonde bombshell', was a lady, a great performer and an artist, who really worked on an audience. She told me a story about travelling to a gig on her own and on arriving at the pub being painfully aware that she was to have major problems with the backing music. Apparently the only melody instrument available to back her was a violin played by a gentleman whose virtuosity didn't encompass the latest chart hits or even the defunct ones. After giving up trying to explain the chords of the songs on the music scores she had brought with her, she told him to forget about the music sheets and asked him simply to give her the key or starting note and then follow her. Eithne got her starting note and went straight into her familiar style of singing, walking among the audience with her radio microphone. It wasn't a particularly funny song she was singing but she noticed that everyone was laughing, and turning around in curiosity, she discovered the fiddle player walking about three feet behind her. Now there was a man who hadn't got an attitude problem, he simply did what he was told.

I didn't have to travel outside Dublin to wind up in hot water at a gig, but in most cases these agonising moments on Dublin stages were my own fault. Always searching for something spectacular to wear, to look really different, I decided to make my own stage costumes. At six o'clock in the morning I put the finishing touches to an outfit that was to cause havoc in the Wexford Inn in Dublin on a packed Saturday night. The outfit consisted of bull fighter's pants to the knees, with a skintight white top caught with a button underneath the bust. A huge fan-shaped collar, a full three feet from side to side and adorned with hundreds of gold sequins, was attached to the top and stood precariously on my shoulders. The collar was rimmed and supported with wire. I was top of the bill and, as Pearse Webb, the popular compère at the Wexford Inn, announced me on stage, I had to bend down carefully to get through my dressingroom door. As I began my opening number, with my head encircled in this huge gold sunburst, it became clear that the big collar was much too heavy for the lighter material of my top. From the weight of the collar, the button under my bust popped out and the big collar fell backwards, dragging my top up over my bust and exposing me. Pearse Webb, who was still on stage, caught the collar and held it up, while I frantically pulled my top back down. After an appeal over the microphone by the compère, five hundred people who had left their homes and paid good money to get into a top cabaret venue to be entertained by a professional artist, were rummaging around looking for a large safety pin to keep the show going.

A skintight leopardskin outfit, something like Paula Yates would wear, gave me a hard time in a sports club in Tallaght. It had no straps but a boned top which gave me the Marilyn Monroe look, from a distance I mean. Everything went well until I came back for an encore and decided to give it that bit extra, kicking my legs high, really doing my nut. The music drowned out the sound of my skintight trousers ripping from just above my backside and continuing down until it could go no further. As I had nothing on underneath, I felt an incoming draught which was quickly followed by the music coming to an unscheduled stuttering halt, and that was accompanied by howls of laughter from the backing group, who saw a side of me they'd never seen before. Seeing my predicament, a man jumped up from the audience and escorted me off the stage, shielding my bare part with two of the biggest hands I've ever seen on a human being, while I just smiled and waved to the crowd. From inside the dressingroom I could hear the crowd roaring and clapping for another encore, but I just opened the door a few inches and shouted out, 'No way!' When the zip broke in the front of my pants on another night in Slatterys of Terenure, a lady gave me her cardigan, which I put around my waist, tying the sleeves at the back, and carried on singing.

I gave up making my own stage clothes because no matter how hard I tried, the clothes always had a homemade look about them. I began to get stage gear made by a professional or bought from the more fashionable shops in Dublin. 'Taffy' Miller was probably the most sought-after outfit-maker in Dublin, and when she made me a coloured body-clinging jumpsuit, it was what it didn't have that turned heads. The entire left leg and right sleeve were missing, and at the time I thought it was sexy and 'with it', but looking back I think I looked like Spiderman emerging from an explosion. Among Taffy Miller's other clients were the all-

135

girl vocal trio, consisting of Maxi, Marian Fossett and Frances Campbell, who were collectively called 'Sheba' and who represented Ireland in the Eurovision Song Contest final in the RDS complex in Dublin, wearing one of Taffy's spectacular designs.

Dermot, our second child, was born on 16 June 1970, giving me a short respite from singing and a chance to think things out musically. In the early 1970s, after my old band, the Cadets, broke up, Jimmy and I were asked to join a band called the Second Sound. The band was formed and managed by the Kelly brothers, Des and Johnny, who used to be part of the Capital Showband. The Second Sound played country music, which was all the rage then, with bands like Big Tom and the Mainliners and the Smokey Mountain Ramblers ruling the musical roost. I made a record at this time called 'I'm Gonna be a Country Girl Again', which got great airplays, giving my image a huge lift. This band didn't last too long, however, and I was soon back to the bread-and-butter cabaret circuit again. I wasn't happy going back to cabaret because I wanted to do a slicker show on stage and keep up with the chart hits, but this was virtually impossible without having my own backing group. In the meanwhile Jimmy, who was a very good singer, was getting work as a compère around Dublin and had a three-nights-a-week residency in the Central Lounge in Balbriggan. Although Jimmy played the saxophone in the Cadets, he was always interested in the guitar, which he played as a hobby. After a lot of discussion about the pros and cons of him learning my programme and joining me on stage, we came to the conclusion that working together was a better long-term idea, even though we were putting all our eggs in one basket. It was a godsend having Jimmy, who not only anchored the show on stage, but was a tremendous asset with his unique voice. I could relax a little now, rehearse slick selections of songs with Jimmy, and go to the gigs knowing that nothing would fall asunder, musically speaking. Our third child, Claudine, completed the family after her birth on 4 April 1973.

In the mid 1970s, cabaret lounges were doing such great business that big international stars such as Guy Mitchell, Marti Caine and Frankie Vaughan, were coming over to perform here. A great double-up venue was the trip on the same night between the huge Drake Inn in Finglas to the Tudor Rooms in the city, which involved fourteen shows over the week's run of engagements. Only the best bands and compères were used in the top lounges, people like Billy Hughes and the DJs in the Drake Inn, and Peter Keegan and the Andy O'Callaghan Band in the Tudor Rooms, Tommy Moloney, Hugh Corr, Joe Cuddy, Billy Vegas, and many more whose talents have stood the test of time.

It wasn't all an old pals' act either, with plenty of good healthy rivalry between artists. Big charity nights held in such places as the Country Club, Portmarnock, or the Drake Inn, always produced problems about who was to go on first, middle, or do the prestigious last spot of the night. There could be up to six or seven top names booked to appear on the bill, and usually most of us would turn up when the second part of the show had started, 'jockeying' for the best 'spot' of the evening. After a couple of occasions when I was rushed into singing two or three songs due to the lateness of the hour, I decided to turn up as early as possible on these big nights, even if it meant going on first. This way I could take my time and do all the songs I wanted to do in front of a guaranteed full house, and then sit back, relax, and watch the squabbles as the acts began to outnumber the minutes left on the clock. My good friend and a great singer, Sonny Knowles, didn't mind what time he went on at, and it didn't really matter either, because Sonny could sing in the car park at two in the afternoon and go a storm.

Performing five and six nights a week in lounges that were springing up like the ballrooms did in the sixties, meant constantly buying clothes for stage, which swallowed up quite a lot of money. I was back so often in places like the Broadstone Inn, Bridget Burke's in Tallaght, the Clare Manor, the Country Club, Meagher's Log Cabin, Rathfarnham Inn, Wexford Inn, Gulliver's Inn, and many many more, including the ill-fated Stardust in Artane, that I couldn't wear the same outfit twice. Years later, when the terrible fire in the Stardust claimed many young lives and caused horrific injuries to so many more, everyone connected with the vast cabaret circuit was deeply shocked and saddened and just couldn't do enough with their talents to help the victims of this tragedy. It is in the aftermath of any tragic event that the deep generosity of entertainers of every kind is brought to the fore, and I have seen over the years the wonderful results of this spontaneous willingness to help.

Home life

With three children now going to school, I was really feeling tired in the mornings trying to get them up, fed, ready and on their way. Jimmy was doing taxi work, mostly at night, so he would be sleeping as the children got up for breakfast. Saint Benedict's primary school was only a five-minute walk away, but I still drove them to and from there as often as peer pressure would allow. It never takes long for a youngster to let the world know that she doesn't need her mother to show her the way home.

Home was located half way down a quiet road, where the houses were built with space and style in mind. These four-bedroomed semis had big gardens back and front and a main entrance to the side facing a car port, which extended to a very substantial driveway. Red brick and grey brick varied the colour in the scheme, young trees were planted on either side of the road, and very low white wooden fencing gave an open, spacious effect. These homes were built before someone got the idea that two houses could be erected on the same area of ground that used to accommodate one, something akin to my toes and shoes arrangement — remember them? Within our view was a lovely little Franciscan church, with open grassland between it and the back gardens of the houses opposite ours. With a railway station ten minutes' walk away, a bus stop at the top of the road, and a shopping centre beside the schools, we were very well situated for modern living.

Our children saw to it that our house was well 'lived in'. Every carpet, armchair, door and wall soon bore the scars of rushing feet, sticky hands, baby walking frames, pets, and every colour and type of spilled liquid you could think of. Luckily I liked decorating, and being the type who has to be doing something, you could find me at all hours of the night either painting, wallpapering or sewing. I found the night-time the best time to work, when everything was still, the children were asleep and there were no distractions. I don't think I was like any normal person — I used to start painting or sewing at twelve midnight and continue until the job was finished, even if it took until six o'clock in the morning. It never surprised any of the family who might happen to be visiting the bathroom in the middle of a particular night to find me wallpapering the landing.

If I didn't surprise them, I certainly surprised a would-be thief at 3 am when he thought that every man, woman and child was sound asleep in bed. I had decided to paint around the hall door and porch and was still working on it at three o'clock in the morning. The door was one that opened inwards, and being positioned at the side of the house, wasn't visible to anyone coming up the driveway. In the quietness of the night, as I stood in the hallway silently stroking the paintbrush, I thought I heard a sound outside. I stepped out under the porchlight and found myself about ten feet from a youth who was sneaking up by the side of the house. He nearly jumped out of his skin with fright, not knowing whether to attack me or run. He chose the latter, and as I calmly walked down to the end of the driveway and looked up the road, I could see him running like a hare and vanishing into a laneway on the other side of the main road. I laughed when I imagined how it must have seemed to him, this prowler of the night stealthily approaching a sleeping household, then suddenly being confronted by this woman popping out of nowhere with a two-inch paintbrush in her hand.

When I started something I just had to finish it, there was no such thing as finishing it tomorrow, and I didn't like taking breaks to make food or even go to the bathroom.

Jimmy went to bed one night and woke to find me painting the ceiling of our bedroom. He was neither surprised nor annoyed, he just shook his head and went back to sleep. The complaints about the smell of paint fell on deaf ears, as I simply opened the windows and let the night or day air whistle through the house. I used my sewing ability to make a lot of the children's clothes when they were toddlers. Matching shirts and shorts for Dermot and little dresses for the girls didn't take that much material and were cheap and easy to make. Every day they went out to play in different varieties of my creations.

I loved the summer time, when Jimmy and I would visit the garden centres, where I liked to potter around at the weekends. If we started working on the garden, Jimmy would call it a day late into the evening, but I would usually carry on till the light faded, and if we had had floodlights, I would probably have still been there at midnight. Gardening gave me my only chance to get a bit of fresh air, and God knows I needed it after singing in smoky pubs during the week. I was never a keep-fit fanatic and wasn't fond of long walks or jogging, but nevertheless I was very healthy.

We did have our share of sickness and accidents, with the worst incident happening to myself. It was around eight o'clock in the morning and I was about to get the children up for school. We had, and still have, the habit of throwing clothes that need washing in a corner on the landing at the top of the stairs. With only a dressing-gown and slippers on, I filled my arms with the customary bundle of clothes and headed downstairs to the washing machine in the kitchen. My feet never got as far as the second step as they, with the help of loose slippers, decided to abandon me, bringing my backside crashing down on the top step. The base of my spine hopped off every step in turn as I bounced downward onto the space where the stairway turned to continue into the diningroom. As I lay on my back half way up the stairs, I was conscious of fluid seeping inside the base of my back. I

141

couldn't move or speak, and then I passed out. Jimmy must have heard the thump as I hit the floor, because when I came to a couple of minutes later, he was kneeling beside me. He got a terrible fright, thinking I was dead or at least paralysed, and after calling an ambulance he very delicately and carefully, so as not to cause any further damage, put on an item of clothing that even if I were dead I wouldn't like to be seen without. Mrs Kelly from across the road kindly offered to look after the house and children when she saw me being wheeled out on a stretcher, but Jimmy stayed at home and left me in the capable hands of the friendly and efficient ambulancemen. Although I was x-rayed and told that there was no serious damage done, I still have to visit an osteopath from time to time, and there is a small circular patch of skin at the bottom of my spine that is permanently white, even after a sunbed session.

On another occasion I was coming home alone by car in the small hours of a winter's morning when, as a result of water spilling from a burst mains and freezing over, my car skidded, turned around a couple of times, hit another car coming in the opposite direction, and then crashed into a wall. The car I was driving at the time was powered by gas and had a large gas tank in the boot. How I wasn't transported from the Howth Road to the roof of nearby Clontarf Castle by a huge explosion I'll never know, because the car was totally wrecked and the lid of the boot torn off. The lethal tank and its pipes seemed to be the only part of the car that wasn't damaged. Even more miraculously, I walked away from the wreck uninjured, despite the fact that I wasn't even wearing a seat belt. Apart from Pamela being hospitalised at one year old with gastroenteritis, Dermot even younger again having a hernia operation, and Claudine breaking her collar bone 'house-playing' with Dermot when she was three, we were thankfully pretty free from major medical worries.

Our pets, all dogs, consisted of 'Pebbles', followed by 'Pebbles — Mark II' and 'Sam', all small breeds who had over the years a selection of wild cats to chase up and down the garden as their only source of exercise, until Jimmy brought them 'walkies' before going out in the taxi at night. I do regret not having been a full-time mammy like my mother, giving my home and the children my undivided attention, instead of trying to build their ordered routine around my irregular abnormal lifestyle. A mother needs a lot of energy to cope successfully with young children, and my energy levels were highest at night-time, leaving me exhausted in the morning, often sleeping on till twelve noon, and sometimes not even having a lunch ready when they came in from school. I had to be a career woman and a mother, and this just didn't work out. I feel today that I fell down with regard to my duties as a mother. Nevertheless, the children were for the most part well fed, well clothed, educated, happy and loved, and besides, what difference did it make whether they had stew or cornflakes for lunch? — most of the time they didn't appreciate it anyway.

She's mad you know

Gerry Daley was the other half of a comic mine act called the Rib Ticklers, and was managing a few cabaret artists, including myself, in the mid 70s. If Gerry suffered from high blood pressure at the time, I would put my name forward as being the main cause of his hypertension. He used to tell me that he was half afraid to ring the owner of the pub where I had been appearing the night before in case I would be the centre of a controversy over what I was wearing, or not wearing! Gerry liked his acts to do things right, wear three-hundred-pound suits, not be seen anywhere on the premises before hitting the stage, and be a model professional at all times. The Hitching Post in Leixlip was his pet venue, and if I was due to sing there he would ring Jimmy and make enquiries as to what I would be wearing. 'Make sure she's not too outrageous or half naked — she's mad you know,' he'd say with a sort of humorous anxiety in his soft Cork accent.

I was always under the impression that the world was moving far too slowly for me. I wanted everything done yesterday, and if I came up with a good idea I found it almost impossible to put it into action because there were so many obstacles put up by unadventurous people and unavailable equipment. When I told Gerry about my idea to stack my hair really high and, with supports, deck it out with coloured fairy lights, he laughed and said that I would either set fire to the place or electrocute myself, and besides, the fellow with the wheelbarrow carrying the battery would take away from my act. When I wanted to be adventurous I came across so many people who just preferred to leave every-

144

thing the way it was. Why couldn't I be like everybody else? I just wasn't, in fact nobody is like anybody else. I was desperately trying to find a new identity — I didn't want to be labelled permanently as a former showband star. Not being on television, big theatre productions or even radio, didn't help, so I had to fight to keep my name to the fore, using a fresh up-to-date 1970s-style stage act to achieve this. I wanted to move with the times, but it was sometimes difficult because people were always asking me to sing songs that I was associated with in the sixties, like 'I Gave My Wedding Dress Away'. When Abba won the Eurovision Song Contest, it gave my cabaret performances a great boost, both musically and visually. I loved the Swedish group, and their blend of terrific songs and dress sense were the perfect ingredients to make a meal of my 'spots' under the lights. I copied everything the girls in Abba wore, and sang all their major hits, perched on top of my silver, knee-length, five-inch-high platform boots, with a scull cap on my newly acquired hairstyle.

Most of the groups around Dublin got used to my programme and there wasn't much hassle with doing my fifty-minute spot, but there were places that I could have done without. The sort of problems here ranged from an unprofessional childish compère wanting to go down better than me with the crowd, thereby making things awkward, to a downright atrocious backing group. An unhelpful compère would make life difficult by leaving the volume and clarity settings on my microphone with a lot to be desired, and on more than one occasion I just had to abandon a quality ballad because the group had gone off in four different directions looking for the chords, which were in front of them.

Dressingrooms, or rather the lack of them, were another bone of contention. There were 'dressingrooms' where, if a cabaret performer left down a pint of lager he was enjoying, and later picked up the wrong glass, he would find himself sampling week-old urine. Picking up a disease on account of the dirt and laziness of the users and owners of these 'dressingrooms' was a real possibility, as was the danger of being burned to death in these junk-infested fire hazards. The last thing that ninety per cent of owners of entertainment venues thought of was a place where the band and artists could change. Nothing elaborate was called for, merely a small room with a mirror, a table and chair, and something to hang a coat on would have made such a difference.

I remember going to do a cabaret spot in a pub about thirty miles south-west of Dublin. When I got there the owner proudly showed me his newly opened upstairs singing lounge. He took me on a grand tour of every corner of it, and although it cost a small fortune he said he was delighted with this beautifully renovated money-spinner. I agreed it was indeed beautiful, wished him luck with it, and then asked if there was a place for me to change. He took me downstairs to the bar, which was full of men. I couldn't believe the difference between the two places, it was indeed a case of 'Upstairs Downstairs'. The bar was a throwback to earlier times, when a drinking man only enjoyed the company of drinking men, and where, if after a severe bout of coughing, the spittoon was missed by a mile, it would be excused because of the poor visibility, due to dense smoke. Then the owner conducted me to a, for want of a better word, 'cubby hole', about fifteen feet from where these 'honest-to-God' drinking men were solving the world's problems. He pulled back this dirty rag, which was supposed to be a curtain, lighted a naked bulb by pulling a piece of string, and said, 'You can change in there.' When I closed over the 'curtain' I discovered that this 'Black hole of Calcutta' slanted away to nothing on one side, making it difficult to stand up except in a small area. The cause of this uncomfortable lack of room was due to the fact that I was underneath a stairway. Can you imagine me trying to strip in a bar full of men with nothing to hide me except a piece of cloth, and trying to put my make-up on, arching my back as

I moved around? I didn't want to walk out like the hunchback of Notre Dame, so I spent as little time as possible there, gathered up all my belongings and went upstairs to the ladies' toilet to put the finishing touches to my make-up. To this day, in the vast majority of singing pubs, I still use the ladies' toilet to change in.

During the hectic days of cabaret in the seventies, I made some good friends among the pub owners and their customers. I had such a rapport with some of the owners when I started handling my own bookings, that we would simply sit down after each Christmas and write into our diaries all my engagements with them for the following year. We had a great mutual understanding which helped if unavoidable changes in plans had to be made on either side. If something really vitally important came up for me and I couldn't fulfil an engagement, they would facilitate me, knowing that I would be equally co-operative with them if the need arose. We were like a big professional family, and things like contracts were never necessary.

With regard to the customers who over the years flocked to cabaret venues to unwind after a hard week's work, I could tell countless stories. These people who constantly crossed my path encompassed the whole spectrum of human types — loud, soft, drunk, sober, annoying, pleasant, awkward, mean, generous, faithful, spiteful, wonderful, hurtful, thoughtful, jealous, happy, sad — all normal working-class people whose support, and love for a good night out, built up a whole new industry, giving employment to so many, including this ex-showband singer who was given a new start after struggling out of the sixties with a name and nothing more. There were those who were one-pub groupies, who went nowhere else on their nights out except to their favourite 'watering hole' and were first in to secure exactly the same seat location on every occasion without fail. There were also those who did a lot more unwinding than others, and if I got 'trapped' by an individual who had, as comedian Sil Fox would say, 'the price of a ton of coal' in him or her, I was really in for an 'ear bashing'. The nostalgic memories of their lives, and indeed of mine, would be narrated, no matter how long it took, despite the fact that their opening statement would be, 'You don't know me but —.' I would be reminded fifty times over about things as obvious as the nose on my face, which by the way I didn't need reminding about, and then for reasons unknown to myself they would take me into their confidence and tell me things that would take great courage to tell in Confession. It's quite amazing and, I suppose, a compliment, the way some people, drunk or sober, often total strangers, would confide in me at a cabaret venue just because I was who I was. I have no idea why I should have merited their trust in this fashion, but their trust was always vindicated. We who performed on stage only saw the happy side of the lives of people we entertained, but everyone, including entertainers, are hit at some time in their lives by sadness, sickness or tragedies.

The most common way of raising money to help victims of misfortunes would be to put on a cabaret show, with the acts giving freely of their services. There was a time in the seventies when I could have worked seven nights a week doing charity shows. I couldn't do this of course, but I, like many others, would commit myself to doing so many. When someone I knew personally was the recipient of much needed help, it brought home to me that I had at my disposal a great means of helping others. It could be said, and indeed has been said, that some cabaret artists just did certain charity shows out of obligation or for appearances' sake. The way Jimmy and I felt about doing these unpaid shows was very simple. All through the years the ordinary people from Finglas and Ballymun on the northside, across to Tallaght and Ballyfermot on the south, and all places in between, who paid to see and support us, were the bread and butter of our lives. It was through their support that we could put food on our table, bring up our children and pay our way through life. We were glad, when we could, and when it was most needed, to give back a little of what we had received.

Small crowd or big crowd, paid or unpaid, every time I went on stage I enjoyed myself and gave it everything I had. There were a couple of occasions when I didn't do what was expected of me in a cabaret venue. I hasten to add that these incidents didn't happen while I was performing on stage. I refer to the art of judging talent competitions, or rather, with regard to these two incidents, the fixing of talent competitions. The services of my good name and impartiality were acquired to be part of a panel of judges on the grand-final night of a talent competition in a large Dublin cabaret venue, which shall be nameless. When the competitors had given their all, I was informed by the organisers of the talent show, that a certain young man who had just competed, was earmarked for success and had a bright future in the business, beginning with dates in the very venue where we judges were about to make our deliberations. This young man who was supposed to receive my enforced vote of confidence may have had a bright future, but he didn't turn on any lights for me, and I was going to give my number one vote to the act which, in my opinion, had won the competition by a 'country mile'. Despite repeated efforts to change my mind, I gave my vote to what I thought was the best performer. Whether my firm stand on the issue was a factor in how the other judges voted, I don't know, but the chap that I gave the 'thumbs up' to, won on the night. His name was David Beggs and he went on to become cabaret's funniest and most successful impersonator. I thought I wouldn't get any more 'gigs' there because of my stubbornness, but there were no hard feelings and we did business as per usual.

At least the organisers in that venue abided by the decision of the judges, but I wasn't so sure about this detail in a different cabaret lounge later. This time it was a beauty contest and the most beautiful girl in the competition in everybody's opinion was left trailing. Again I was asked to vote for a particular competitor and again I said no. The girl in question was not the best-looking contestant, and anybody with an eye in their head could see this. Nevertheless, she was given first place, despite the fact that I and at least a couple of other judges didn't vote for her. Some of the girls in the audience that night, who also thought it was the wrong decision, afterwards said to my face that I was just jealous of the girl who should have won. Little did they know that I hadn't actually voted for the selected winner. Ah well, you can't win them all.

You ain't heard nothing yet

*I*t was while I was doing a charity show in the bar of the Olympia Theatre that I met director Noel Pearson, who had tremendous success with the long-running show *Jesus Christ Superstar* in 1973 at the Gaiety Theatre. Also at the charity show I met an old friend, Earl Gill, and a girl called Amy Hayden who sang with Earl in a country band aptly named The Hoedowners, and they were chatting with Noel Pearson. I said hello to Noel and jokingly enquired if there was any chance of me getting into one of his shows. 'You'd be too expensive,' he answered. 'Try me,' I replied, adding that I would be willing to start at the bottom, even just pulling the curtains on stage. 'Well, we'll see' were Noel's last words to me as I left their company.

Singer Tony Kenny was packing the pubs at this time as a result of his huge success in *Jesus Christ Superstar*, and it was at one of his cabaret performances that I was to meet Noel Pearson again. If Jimmy and I were going out together for a night, he never insisted on going anywhere in particular and would be happy enough no matter where we went. On this particular Sunday night I was going to go to the Tudor Rooms to see Tony Kenny and possibly meet Noel Pearson, who was his manager. I later changed my mind and decided I'd stay at home, but Jimmy said, 'No! We're going to the Tudor Rooms.' I still wasn't keen to go, but uncharacteristically Jimmy insisted, and so we went. After the show, and on the way out of the cabaret lounge, I met Noel, who informed me that auditions were being held for a new show to be staged in the Gaiety Theatre in 1976, called *You Ain't Heard Nothing Yet*. He went on to warn me not to be too disappointed if I was unsuccessful, as all the top girl-dancers and singers were competing for parts. I told him I didn't mind and was not afraid of rejection.

I saw some familiar faces coming and going from the ballroom of the Shelbourne Hotel where the auditions were taking place, and I also saw Noel himself there, encouraging and consoling many of the hopeful females. I had the music of the songs I was going to sing with me, but they were not the ones Noel suggested, because I just couldn't see myself singing a Sophie Tucker number. I had listened to an LP of Sophie which I had borrowed from Danny Cummins, and came to the conclusion that Ethel Merman was more up my street. 'Oh, great,' I thought, as I spotted Chris Kenevey sitting to attention at his piano waiting to accompany me as I tried to convince a large bald American director that I was good enough to be picked for Noel's play. Chris was a friend of mine who wrote some music scores for me in the past and would be very familiar with my opening audition effort, Edith Piaf's 'No Regrets'. Although there were only two cleaners working at the back of the ballroom, I belted out the song as if I was in a packed Carnegie Hall. The director smiled all through my performance, probably thinking, 'This one doesn't hold back anything, does she.' He clapped when I finished and asked if I had anything else prepared. When I showed him a short list, he picked Barbara Streisand's 'Second Hand Rose' and said, 'Do that one.'

Noel Pearson had warned me beforehand not to forget any of my lines because it would go against me, but I was to prove him wrong in this. As I sang the song I walked around the director's chair, using him as a prop, as if he was the object of all my movements. His eyes followed me around the chair, and I totally forgot where I was in the song, and continued on with my own words and a few la las, putting even more energy into the improvised bit. When I had finished, he checked with Chris on the piano to see what sort of vocal range I had, and when I had sang a few scales he turned to me and said, 'Did you know that you have a bastard voice.' It was lucky I heard the whole sentence clearly or I would have thought I'd lost the spot in the show. I didn't know whether to say yes or no in case it might jeopardise my chances, so I just looked at him innocently and said, 'Really!' Apparently I possessed the ability to change the sound of my voice and imitate other singers.

Even though I was happy with the way the audition went, I wasn't really expecting the phone call that announced that I was to appear in my first musical extravaganza on a theatre stage. In order to cast me in the most appropriate role, I had to be vocally scrutinised by another wonderful director and gentleman, the late Alan Simpson. Alan asked me if he could see me perform somewhere, and although I would have loved to have said 'Drop in to the Metropolitan Opera House', I took a deep breath and replied, 'Sure, I'm up in the Brown Derby singing pub in James's Street near the Guinness Brewery on Saturday night.' After listening to me go through my raucous programme in the James's Street pub, he confidently assured me that the Ethel Merman type numbers were indeed 'up my street'.

Throughout the run of *You Ain't Heard Nothing Yet*, my raspy voice could be heard belting out that great standard 'I've Got Rhythm'. I was in a different world now, with a new circle of friends, I was with the 'in' people. I was wondering how I would be accepted into this élite fold, because Noel Pearson had told me that my inclusion in the show raised a few eyebrows. 'Who!' was one of the most used exclamations when my name came up in answer to the enquiries about the final selections. After all, I was only a pub singer. I needn't have worried. I was accepted without reserve by everybody, from the very friendly director/choreographer of the show, Domy Reiter-Soffer, right through the entire cast, which included Tony Kenny, Noel Purcell, Maxi, Amy Hayden, Cecil Sheridan, Fran Dempsey and Pat Reilly. Pat was part of a very popular singing duo called 'Pat and Jean', and later they both became lifelong friends. I was also to work with Domy Reiter-Soffer many years later when he directed a play called *Mary Makebelieve* in the Gate Theatre.

After the opening night of *You Ain't Heard Nothing Yet* in the Gaiety, Noel Pearson asked for my spot to be lengthened, and told Sadie Looney, the wardrobe mistress, to cut the sides of my leotard so I would show legs up to my waist instead of having them looking like a 1940s bathing suit. The show was a real top hat and tails, high-kicking song and dance affair, and was a great success. The excitement of it all overwhelmed me, and although the work was tough, I enjoyed it immensely and lived for the after-show happy party atmosphere in the Green Room later on. I got to like this exciting company so much that I hated going home. Up to now I had never been a drinker, and if I took a couple of mouthfuls of lager to clear my throat before doing a cabaret gig with Jimmy, that was as much as I would drink for the night. After every cabaret show, Jimmy and I always went home, we never stayed back to drink and never wanted to. The scene that I was in now was totally different than working in cabaret and a million miles from being on the road with the Cadets, which was hard slogging, unattractive and unglamorous. This was the good life where, after the 'high' of being on stage, people relaxed, had fun, a few drinks and enjoyed themselves. After one glass of Guinness I would feel tipsy, after two I would really feel good, happy, loving the world, kissing everybody, bringing the love part of my feelings to the fore. If I had four glasses of beer I could have been enticed to bed with very little encouragement.

Up to this time in my career I had been, on more than one occasion, propositioned by good-looking young men, but I never was tempted. I was married and it would be wrong, it was a no-go area and it ended there. But I was in a completely different world now, a world in which I felt free, without responsibilities, able to express myself, living life to the full without seeing any harm in it. The first night the show travelled outside Dublin, and after a few 'after-show' drinks, I felt happy, loving, and found myself in bed with a male who probably felt the same as I did. This one-night-stand led to more with different partners, each of us just using the other to finish off a night of fun with sex. I was never into anything sordid like trying to take anyone's husband or boyfriend away from them, or even forming a relationship. I just enjoyed partying, meeting different people, having fun, and getting a buzz from the few drinks that erased any inhibitions to occasionally do what I knew I shouldn't. It was all fun as far as I was concerned, no seedy love scenes, just lovey dovey into bed and thanks for the memory. I didn't have any pretences about being a sex symbol, woman's gift to men, or even looking for a rating from one to ten on the sex scale. I could now see how easy it was to fall into this casual sex thing and could also see that it would never have started without me being under the influence of alcohol. I didn't like it when the show ended, I just wanted this high life to go on twenty-four hours a day, and I couldn't face the drudgery of housework and worrying about paying bills and staying in at night.

I was delighted when Noel Pearson offered me the part of an ugly sister in a production of *Cinderella* in Goffs in Naas, just outside Dublin. Johnny Logan, who was to win the Eurovision Song Contest twice for Ireland, and his brother Michael, as well as Alma Carroll, who also represented Ireland with Nicola Kerr and the Swarbrigg brothers, starred in the show, and Jean Swift played opposite me as the other ugly sister. Earl Gill and his band provided the music, and we were all one big happy family. Jean and I were very 'off the wall' ugly sisters, jumping around the place like clowns and enjoying the whole carnival atmosphere of a really zany Christmas panto. When each performance was finished, the cast would be joined by friends, and these numbers would be increased by others I'd never met, and before long everyone would be partying. It wouldn't be long before I would get 'tipsy', and on the odd occasion catch the eye of someone who would make the night complete. Earl Gill, who was like a father figure to me, and whom I admired as a very genuine person and friend, used to shake his head at me and say, 'My God, Reid, after two you'd be anybody's', knowing that I just couldn't handle drink. My fellow artists were like a family to me, and even today they are all still very good friends. But as each show passed, I was going further and further away from my real family. It became awkward at home, I just wanted to be out all the time enjoying myself. Between big shows I did cabaret gigs with Jimmy, but during all this time Jimmy did his own gigs and took care of the children. During the rehearsals and the run of *You Ain't Heard Nothing Yet*, Claudine was only three years old, and Jimmy had to look after her most of the day and night.

After the show in the Gaiety, I got to know Alan Amsby, better known as Mr Pussy, a very successful drag artist both here and in England. Alan was staging an 'adult' pantomime called *Cinderfella* in Gulliver's Inn, a public house in New Street, about three hundred yards from my old home in Patrick Street. He asked me to play the prince in a cast that boasted the talents of some of Dublin's best-known cabaret acts, including comedian Sil Fox, the great voice of Eric Murrey, Mr Pussy himself, and character actor Freddy Davonport. We were all very surprised to see among the audience on opening night, Maureen Potter, Ursula Doyle, Fred O'Donovan and Danny Cummins from the Gaiety Theatre. We had no idea why these illustrious people should grace us with their presence, but they did, and they thoroughly enjoyed themselves. Maybe they thought this was a threat and the future of panto was to be in the atmosphere of the public house, where people could enjoy the Christmas spirit in more ways than one. If this was the case, these fears were groundless, because nothing compares with a traditional children's pantomime performed in theatres such as the Gaiety and the Olympia. *Cinderfella* went to other pubs and enjoyed a successful run, and Alan followed this with a summer show called *Hello Duckies*, which I also took part in. Alan and I became very good 'walking out' friends, with absolutely no sexual relationship involved. We enjoyed each other's company without the hassle of any commitment. We also enjoyed going to night clubs such as Suzy Street, or maybe to the theatre or other variety shows. The Trocadero restaurant was a favourite haunt where we could talk till the small hours of the morning. We went anywhere there was excitement, anywhere we could stay out all night.

Side by Side by Sondheim was being produced at the Gaiety in 1977, starring Gemma Craven and also, as narrator, Gay Byrne. I was offered one of the supporting roles, but unfortunately I had to go into hospital to have a node removed from my vocal chords. I met Gay afterwards and he said I would have loved being involved in the show, which he obviously thought was a great experience for himself. I certainly would have enjoyed *Side by Side* because I was desperately looking for bigger and better parts in shows just to keep my name to the fore and stay in the top bracket of the Irish entertainment scene. I wanted to be a bigger name, naturally, to make money, but also to keep up the exciting lifestyle and late-night socialising. At this time there were big receptions and opening nights that I wanted to be present at but was not far enough up the social ladder to receive an invite. When I was not appearing in a show, I still went out at night and dropped in to where there would be something happening, even it if was just for a chat or a drink or a meal, anything to brighten up my life until I was involved in the next big production.

The late nights and the occasional fling continued, and I began at this stage to realise that there was something missing in my life. I wasn't fulfilled, all this was just surface happiness, and I wondered, 'Is this what life is really all about?' I wasn't into religion, and as far as that was concerned, I thought I knew what I had to know. I just wasn't getting the satisfaction out of my life that I felt I should have. I had thought I was on the right road, that the secret of success and happiness was having influential friends, fame and money, followed by partying and very late nights, without any thought of who might be hurt, and marriage unfaithfulness just a minor detail. As far as I was concerned, male company from time to time was better than doing nothing, it kept the night going and never involved any lasting relationship or even close friendship; I was just using them and they were using me.

On one occasion I was so bored that I decided to get away from everything, and went on a holiday on my own. I couldn't even afford it, but I got the money together, dumped the kids on Jimmy, and flew to Tenerife. I knew it was an awful thing to do, but I couldn't help it. I had no plan in my life, nothing to keep me occupied, I just didn't know where I was at. I was like a child in a playpen who, after getting all the toys available, got tired of them, didn't want them anymore, and became restless. When I got to Tenerife I knew I had made a mistake and wanted to come home again. I stayed, burned myself badly in the sun, and got so frustrated that I thought I was having a nervous breakdown. Being alone, I was 'chatted up' and could have 'carried on', but I just wasn't interested, I wanted to go home. The most important thing for me now was to keep my head, be strong, and above all, not to crack up.

When I got home from the holiday, I considered the situation I was in, and came to terms with what was happening to me. I knew there were thousands of families with the same sort of problem as ours, and that some of the solutions tried, left them in an even worse predicament. I didn't love my husband and wanted to be away from him at all costs, but at the same time I had a responsibility to the children. There were, however, a few pluses in the sorry affair. I knew that I would never look for a separation or go and live with someone else and take the children with me, and also, although Jimmy had his doubts about my faithfulness, he was still in love with me, so we never fought or shouted or even raised our voices at each other in anger, leaving the children peacefully unaware of what was happening in our unsteady relationship. I decided that no matter what decision I made, the welfare of the children would come first. If I wanted to mess up my own life, that was fair enough, but I couldn't destroy five lives no matter how unpleasant the remedy would be for me. I didn't hate Jimmy, I just fell out of love with him. I didn't want to be with him or go anywhere in his company, but I would live with him for the sake of the children. Although I was never to form any serious relationship outside my marriage, my love of excitement and night life was to lead to my almost total undoing.

Crisis at home

When I missed my period and was well into the second month, I got worried and went to my local doctor, who, after doing some simple tests, pole-axed me with two words, 'You're pregnant'. This was a horrific discovery, as I wasn't having sex with Jimmy at the time and he was sure to know that it was not his child. I was in a terrible state and didn't know what to do. I had been in many 'scrapes' in my life, but this one 'took the biscuit'. Abortion came into my head, but it wasn't a big news topic then and I hadn't a clue what it entailed or even where it could be done. I never dreamed of going for professional help or advice, I just wanted nobody to know, but I realised I would have to confide in somebody, and soon. So I walked into the house one day and told Jimmy everything. It must have been the last straw for him because he told me three things: one, he was not going to rear someone else's child; two, if I got myself into this predicament, I could get myself out of it; and three, if I didn't, he would throw me and my belongings onto the street and be finished with me, and then he walked away.

I was devastated and cried continually for the rest of the day. One of the magazines that I read was *Cosmopolitan*, and it was at the back of this that I found the telephone number of an abortion clinic in London. I rang, and a very pleasant lady's voice said, 'Hello, can I help you?', as if she was the receptionist in the office of a business firm. 'It's simple,' she said, 'just come over and the "service" will be performed on one day, and you can go home on the next.' She also pointed out that it didn't hurt and was quite safe. I've forgotten what the price was but as I put the phone down I got a strong feeling that something was wrong with this whole idea. It was a way out for me, but somehow I believed it was not the solution to my problem. I felt miserable again, my back was to the wall and my world was falling apart. I was crying on my own in our bedroom, saying over and over, 'O God, what am I going to do? O God, O God', when suddenly it hit me, 'that's it, God, that's where I'll go.'

We had only one religious picture in the house and that was of the Sacred Heart, which was given to us by fans from the north of Ireland as a wedding present. It was hanging in Claudine's room, and I ran in and got down on my knees in front of it. As I looked up at the image of the face of Christ I burst out crying and pleaded, 'What will I do?' Then I said in all sincerity to God, 'I won't get rid of the baby, I'll have it and leave the rest to you. You control it from here, and even if I get thrown out of the house, I'll have the baby. I'll do whatever you want, leave it in your hands, and whatever happens to me, I will accept it.' I got up from the floor and felt relieved, as if someone else was now going to look after everything. I don't know why I said what I said while I was on my knees, but that's the way it came out.

The next day and in consequence of the presence of an ominous blood stain, I walked to the doctor's surgery close by, and after an examination he told me that I had had a miscarriage. When I asked him what was the cause of it, he enquired if I had fallen heavily or done anything extremely strenuous. I said I hadn't, and he just couldn't give me an explanation for what happened. He said I was a perfectly healthy woman, who never had a miscarriage before, and he could see no physical reason for it. I knew the reason. God had answered my prayer. The relief was unbelievable. If this had happened to anybody else I know it would have turned them into a saint. This ungrateful brat, however, didn't even thank God, but rather vowed to be more careful in the future. I didn't think I had to give God back anything in thanksgiving; after all, he was there to help when it was really needed, and it was no trouble to someone with his powers. I was supposed to be a Catholic, and up to the time when this crisis occurred, I was practising, going to Mass with Jimmy and the children every Sunday, but now I had clearly lost my way spiritually, ironically coinciding with my newfound lifestyle.

Jimmy was visibly very relieved when I told him what the doctor said, but he repeated his ultimatum with regard to me being kicked out of the house. One of his very adamant conditions, one that I had to promise to obey, unless I wanted to walk the streets or live with my mother, was that I would finish totally with 'playing around'. I made every promise under the sun, and kept none of them. I went back to my old ways, but this time I was clever and made sure to protect myself. My unfaithfulness became part of my life, like having a drink or a chat, but on these now rare occasions of out-of-wedlock intimacy, I made sure not to make the same mistake again. I was getting on very well with Jimmy now, and although I felt guilty about being unfaithful to him, the part of my life that he didn't know about became a very normal thing for me to do. I was 'bubbly' and extrovert on the outside, but unhappy and unfulfilled on the inside, and a hypocrite to boot.

Jimmy, in his efforts to come to terms with my restlessness, and having no idea that I was unfaithful, tried to get me to go to Mass, but I told him I couldn't, I would have to want to do something before I did it, and I didn't want to go to Mass. How could a person like me, living a lie, go to a place where truth is the centre of things. You may ask why, if I was so restless and unhappy, didn't I give up my loose living, and my answer at the time would have been, because I had nothing better to replace it with. Although I had a good husband, three lovely children and my health, the ordinary day-to-day home life wasn't moving fast enough for me. I was working hard, and all I was doing was making a modest living and paying bills. I wanted to see something for my hard work, I wanted to buy clothes for myself and have a good time. Any money I was making, and it was by no means great, seemed to vanish. I would have to give a week's earnings for a stage outfit, and then replace it with monotonous regularity. I couldn't save a penny and lost interest in the economics of running a household. Sometimes I would get so uptight that I'd get the price of a holiday together and go off on my own or with some friends. If I did accumulate a few quid, I would rather splash out on an expensive dress than pay urgent bills. The only kick I got out of earning money was spending it, and the best way I liked spending it was on really nice clothes. If I had been earning a fortune, I would never have hoarded it, this was not in my nature, and the money I was making just wasn't enough to keep a home going and indulge in the buying sprees that would at least make the hard work worthwhile. Jimmy and I continued working in cabaret, and I kept my sanity by having my nights out or working alone in the occasional show that came along.

From song contests to pantomimes

The ten years of the seventies neither saw the resurrection or the demise of my career. I just about held on to what I had, mainly by personally slogging around the Dublin pubs and making a rare appearance in the theatre. As far as the rest of Ireland was concerned, I might as well have been retired and living on the 'millions' I was supposed to have made in the sixties. One of the rare TV spots I got, featured me taking off a fictitious Dublin character called Lizzie Leonard. I had recorded a song called 'Lizzie Leonard', written by Des Smyth, a great singer as well as television and recording star. It wasn't the sort of song I particularly liked, being an old time waltz with comedy lyrics, but strangely enough, it opened up a different road in my career. I was looking for a pop song or a good country song as a means of getting back into the Irish charts and maybe forming a small band and touring like I did in the sixties. But finding songs, making demonstration records, getting musical arrangements done, and trying to promote myself on my own, was burning up money that I couldn't afford. Managements weren't really interested in me because they regarded me as a spent force who made it once and wouldn't again.

It was while performing Lizzie Leonard in character on stage that I discovered comedy came very naturally to me, and this was later to be my saving grace. I had always thought that singing was the only way forward for me, and had never considered options like acting, comedy or even songwriting. My first venture into the latter happened after I had noticed that Jimmy had been dabbling in writing poetic lyrics. When

I read some of them I was very impressed, but he seemed to be into writing lyrics only and didn't put any music to them. I started to compose melodies while I was doing things around the house, like making the beds or washing the dishes, and eventually I tried out one of my melodies with Jimmy's lyrics. If the tune I hummed conflicted with his lyric flow, he would simply write around the tune until the whole thing jelled. Our first completed effort was called 'The Saddest Show on Earth', and we entered it in the National Song Contest in 1980. We recorded the song with the help of my friends Pat Reilly and Adele King, who did backing vocals, and listening to the finished product gave us a big thrill.

To our great delight 'The Saddest Show on Earth' was picked as one of the eight finalists in the National Song Contest to be televised on RTE. Things were looking up at last. From being almost forgotten, I was now about to sing my own song in the national final of the biggest song contest in the world. Bill Whelan, a wonderful musician who was later to compose the world-famous *Riverdance*, had helped tremendously with getting the song from my head on to paper and then recorded. He loved the song and was hoping that he would be picked to arrange it for the National final. Eight different arrangers were chosen for each of the final songs. Bill was picked to arrange Shay Healy's 'What's Another Year', and a marvellous jazz pianist, Jim Doherty, was selected for ours.

I had a bit of a scare during the run-up to the final, when Jimmy and I met Tom McGrath of RTE, who was producing the show. He asked Jimmy who he wanted to sing our song and Jimmy said he wanted me to sing it. Mr McGrath asked who was singing on the recording, and when I said it was me, he seemed to have doubts, and asked if I could sing it straight away in front of others at the meeting. I sang the song and, still addressing Jimmy, Tom offered a selection of top Irish female singers to perform our entry on National final night. We preferred to stick with our original plan, so

165

McGrath finally gave me the OK to compete as singer and songwriter. Later, as was customary, he ran a book on the outcome of the National final. Anyone connected with the running of the show, like technicians, musicians, camera operators, would bet on their favourite song and get odds from Tom. Our song was firm favourite with the punters and I was quietly confident that we were in with a great chance of winning.

Dave Pennefeather, an old showband colleague, was involved in a major way in a record company, and it would have been to our mutual advantage if 'The Saddest Show on Earth' was successful. Dave was sitting among the press representatives who were covering the show, and when I had finished singing on the big night, he came running down to me with the news that the press were of the opinion that I had it won. I was just beginning to think that 1980 was going to be a very special year, when Johnny Logan stepped up and sang 'What's Another Year', and turned it into just another year. Johnny went on to win the Eurovision Song Contest with this Shay Healy composition, and I went back to the drawing board. At least Tom McGrath made a few bob that night, with the favourite beaten into fourth place. 'The Saddest Show on Earth' was released, got a few airplays and then disappeared.

We got great encouragement from the favourable reaction to our first song, so we kept writing and entering song contests. Outside of the National Song Contest, the most popular competition for Irish composers, and indeed for writers from abroad, was the Castlebar International Song Contest. The quarter-finals and semi-finals of this west-of-Ireland musical extravaganza were held over several nights in the Traveller's Friend Hotel in Castlebar, and the final televised by RTE. Our songs featured in several of the semi-finals over the years, and although we never reached the final, we really enjoyed the novelty of it all. Berger paints were the sponsors and they looked after everyone in the contest very well, from the opening reception announcing all the finalists, right through to the final itself. Jimmy and I wrote a song about Mother Teresa of Calcutta and it reached the semi-finals in Castlebar. It featured a choir from the town and sounded really good until an American gentleman, who was one of the adjudicators, said that it wouldn't be popular if released as a record because nobody in America knew who Mother Teresa was, including himself. Shay Healy, who had some good songs in the competition over the years, described our Mother Teresa song as 'Close encounters of the Third World'. Shay was always a great 'one line' artist, but this American adjudicator must have been living on a remote Indian reservation if he never heard of Mother Teresa.

The years of entering these competitions, despite their ups and downs, were by and large a happy and exciting time. I always applied a positive attitude to each venture, and all the preparations and publicity hype burned up my high energy. I lived off hope. Here was something that could change everything, I was in the public eye, even if I was making no money from it. Publicity costs were high, as it was often necessary to make demonstration records, prepare music arrangements for orchestra, and in some cases, have a recording of the song released. As well as this, the stage outfits, which for me at least had to be glittery, very special, and different on each night of the competition, were expensive. Despite the expense, I was busily doing what I liked best, involved with high-profile showbusiness and all its glamour.

During these years, Jimmy was working with me as co-writer of the songs. We travelled to the competitions, attended the receptions, and generally enjoyed the occasions together. We were a professional team and had a lot in common, sharing our love for the stage, songwriting and the music business in general. We were also very compatible, and it was more to the credit of our compatibility that things were as normal as possible at home. The years didn't change me, I continued to be unfaithful, but all the while very discreetly, making sure I would never be caught out again. Jimmy trusted me, but though he never suspected any infidelity, he must have known that his obvious love for me was one-sided. In 1981 he got himself a day job working as a traffic warden with the Department of Justice and started spending more time writing lyrics. He never liked late-night clubs and was outside the circle of my showbusiness friends, but he understood that I liked to meet them occasionally and also that these meetings were always late-night affairs. Things continued year after year in an atmosphere of excitement, disappointment, a sprinkling of humour, a lot of tolerance, but never as far as I was concerned, of mutual love. We brought the children to a couple of the out-of-town competitions whenever we reached the finals, such as the Cavan International and Mitchelstown Cheese Song Contest. In Cavan we stayed with a cousin of Jimmy's, Maura O'Shea, and her husband Lynus. They must have brought us luck because we won a beautiful piece of Cavan crystal for reaching third place on final night.

One trip I will never forget was the journey to the Tipperary Song Contest. One of our songs reached the final and Jimmy and I headed off by car for Tipperary town, complete with my stage gear and music arrangements. Fortunately, the children weren't with us. When we reached the outskirts of Naas, our car made some terrible noises and stopped dead. After looking under the bonnet, Jimmy came to the correct conclusion that the engine had seized. Although the car was checked before we left, a faulty warning light failed to inform us of a loss of oil. We had bought the car a couple of months previously for nine hundred pounds, it being all we could afford, and as the saying goes, 'you get what you pay for'. So here we were about eighty miles from our destination, with clothes and bags, standing at the side of the road, with steady rain completing the sorry picture. We thought we could get a train from Naas, and so we walked to the station, which

 Contd p185

*25. Eileen at the opening of her hairdressing salon in
Aungier Street, Dublin, 1966.*

*26. Larry Gogan presents the Pye Records Golden
Guinea Award to Eileen, 1965.*

27. *Eileen with some young fans at the Iveagh Baths, 1965.*

28. *The Cadets had a monster hit with 'I Gave My Wedding Dress Away' in 1964, and Eileen wore this wedding dress on stage in ballrooms and marquees the length and breath of Ireland. A replica was later raffled to raise money for the Central Remedial Clinic.*

29. Eileen and Jimmy at their first dress dance in the Palm Beach Hotel, Portmarnock, 1963.

30. *The Cadets arriving at Kennedy Airport for an American tour, 1963.*

31. Jimmy and Eileen on their wedding day, 24 June 1968.

32. Eileen on her wedding day with her father, Charlie, and bridesmaids (left to right) Helen Day (Jimmy's sister), Kitty and Beatrice (Eileen's sisters).

33. Children Pamela and Dermot, 1971.

34. Eileen and Jimmy on the cabaret circuit, 1970s.

35. You Ain't Heard Nothing Yet, *Gaiety Theatre, 1976. (Left to right, standing) Pat Reilly, Maxi, Amy Hayden, with Eileen seated.*

36. Jack and the Beanstalk *panto, written and directed by Eileen and Jimmy, 1986. (Left to right) Helen Jordan, Eileen, Alan Amsby (Mr Pussy) and Sonny Knowles.*

37. Cabaret in Mosney Theatre, 1980s.
Eileen with Mr Pussy (Alan Amsby) centre, and cabaret colleagues
Vicky (left) and Sally (right).

38. *The cast of* Nunsense, *Olympia Theatre, 1984. (Left to right, standing) Joan Brosnan-Walsh, Eileen, Joan O'Hara, Fiona Douglas-Stuart, Brona Mullen, (kneeling) Candy Devine and Fiona Sinnot.*

39. Eileen as the fairy godmother in Sleeping Beauty
at the Gaiety Theatre, 1986.

40. June Rodgers and Eileen as Scarlet and Charlotte in Cinderella,
Gaiety Theatre, 1994.

41. Eileen as Mrs Lovett in a scene from Sweeney Todd, *directed by Michael Scott, at the National Concert Hall, 1994. The other actors are Paul Monaghan (standing) and Declan Sheridan.*

42. Eileen and Jimmy, with their children (left to right) Pamela, Claudine and Dermot, 1995.

wasn't too far. Unfortunately, the next train wasn't due for several hours, so we decided to hitch. I knew for the first time what it was like to be desperate for a lift and watch car after car speed past. A couple of motorists did stop, but they weren't going very far, so our progress was slow. Just as we were getting worried about the time, along came a huge haulage truck which, to our surprise, pulled in alongside us. The young man driving the truck said he could take us to within a few miles of Tipperary town. We couldn't believe our luck as we climbed into the high cab, very grateful to be off the road and in from the rain.

The driver, who was on his way home after a trip to Italy, left us about five miles from our destination. We had just said goodbye to him when a small car pulled up with about four members of the travelling community inside. 'Are ye goin' to the contest, Sir,' one of them said. We said we were, but couldn't see how we could fit into this small car. 'Get in, there's plenty a room', we were told, as we squashed ourselves, our clothes and bags in beside these kindly travellers of the road. The driver took off like a scalded cat, excitedly talking and looking at us at the same time, only glancing out at the twisting road for long enough to negotiate bends, during which we were all thrown to one side and then the other. I felt like I was part of a Mr Magoo cartoon, with the car just about going where it was supposed to. It was just as well I had nothing to eat all day because my stomach wanted to leave my body almost as much as I wanted to leave the car.

We were taken right to the hall where the competition was held, and after struggling out of the car, we walked into the auditorium, tired, hungry, damp and dispirited. The first person we met was Dessie Reynolds, the drummer with the orchestra, and when we related to him what had happened to us, he cheered us up no end by saying, 'What do you expect from a car that cheap? I wouldn't drive it across town, let alone to Tipperary, to where everyone knows is a long way.' Despite the setbacks I enjoyed taking part in the show, which was compèred by my good friend, RTE producer Kevin Hough. We didn't win anything, and after staying overnight in Tipperary, Kevin drove us back to Naas and then towed our 'banger' back to Dublin, where he also lived.

Trying to keep my image alive and my career moving was costing almost as much as I was making. I just couldn't stop trying, and at the same time the strain of going nowhere and having nothing was getting to me. Endeavouring to get major things done without the money to pay for them was becoming a cross that had to be borne, because these things were an absolute must if I was to stand any chance of surviving musically. I know people were under the impression that I was 'loaded' and terribly mean, but that wasn't the case, I just didn't have it. Trying to stay in the big league meant the money was going into one hand and out the other. I couldn't give the impression that I had nothing either, otherwise I would get nothing done. There were times when I felt like screaming, maybe joining a touring circus, even cleaning up after the elephants, just to get away from it all.

I always felt comfortable doing auditions. I was never nervous and always gave my all. Come to think of it, I was far more successful with auditions than I was in song contests. A good audition got me the part of Sister Robert-Ann in *Nunsense* in the Olympia, alongside some great troupers such as Candy Devine and Joan O'Hara. I always felt very 'at home' in theatre variety because I could sing and act and generally have fun without any feeling that it was work. A typical example of really having a ball playing a part on stage was when I got the part of a trumpet-blowing stripper in the musical *Gypsy* at the Gaiety Theatre. I played the character Mazeppa and was given the task of singing a great song called 'You Gotta Get a Gimmick', and then blowing a bugle all over the place, including between my legs.

I would have said I could fly an aircraft to get a part in a good musical, I would literally try anything, and nine times out of ten my enthusiasm would pull me through. At the auditions for parts in Gypsy, in which Rosaleen Linehan, one of our best-known actresses, played the lead part of Rose, I met Fred O'Donovan, the managing director of the Gaiety Theatre, Miss Billy Barry, who was and still is the 'queen of the dancing school' in Dublin, and Graham Ripley, the musical director of the show. I was informed by Graham when he put me through my paces for the part of Mazeppa, that over the years the particular number that I would have to sing had played havoc with the voices of practically every artist who ever performed it over a long run of the show. When I followed his instructions to sing as loud and as hard as I possibly could, he then asked if I could do that every night for several weeks. I told him that if I could survive six nights a week roaring my head off in every ballroom in the country, with drums beating behind me, guitars in one ear and brass in the other, I think I could handle 'You Gotta Get a Gimmick'. When he asked if I could play the trumpet I thought he was joking, but, straightfaced, I told him no, but that I would learn. He laughed, believed me, recommended me for the part and left the trumpet to my enthusiasm.

I hadn't the faintest idea how to play a trumpet, or a bugle, as it turned out to be. The first thing I had to do was to get one and try it. I made my way up to Waltons' music store in North Frederick Street, not far from O'Connell Street, and enquired about purchasing a bugle. The assistant presented me with this little piece of metal costing twenty-nine pounds, with nothing on it to press or push, and I got the strange feeling that I had bitten off more than I could blow. I asked if there was somewhere I could 'try it out' and was directed to a quiet corner of the shop. The corner remained quiet because, despite blowing until my face turned every colour of the rainbow, I couldn't get any sound out of it. I panicked and headed for Neary's pub in Chatham Street, which has a back entrance a few feet from the stage door of the Gaiety Theatre. I knew that some of the musicians from the theatre would be quenching their thirst there, and was hoping to contact my trumpet-playing friend Earl Gill. Earl wasn't there, but I was lucky enough to find another fine trumpet player, Mike Nolan, who was destined to solve my problem. I showed Mike the bugle and said, 'I can't blow this thing, and I told Graham Ripley that I would play it in *Gypsy*.' 'Show me what you are doing,' said Mike, and I proceeded to inflate my face instead of the inside of the bugle. 'No,' said Mike, 'you're supposed to spit into it.' He showed me this 'spitting' technique, and when I tried it on the bugle, a big 'rasp' came out. I was delighted, I thanked Mike and made my way home to practise.

When I started to blow it in the house there was murder. The kids kicked up a fuss because they couldn't hear their 'ghetto blasters' with the noise I was making, so I blew it out through the open back window. We had a dog named Sam at the time, and he was too heavy and short-legged to get rid of the cats who used to perch themselves on our back-garden walls. The cats just ignored Sam's barking and running up and down, but when I sounded reveille out through the window, every cat disappeared as if the redcoats and hounds had arrived. I practised until I could actually pitch the cavalry charge that I was to blow in my spot in *Gypsy*, and when I performed it on stage the band were knocked out with my efforts. Mike Nolan, playing in the 'pit' band, was on standby to blow my part on trumpet in case I got a fit of the giggles or my mouth went dry. There were nights when it sounded like the final few notes at Custer's last stand, but in most of the performances I blew it in perfect pitch, to the noisy delight of the band.

Jane Russell's famous big bra, designed by Howard Hughes in the 1940s, wasn't a patch on the monster bust-supporter I had to wear in *Gypsy*. Although I was extremely well-endowed, I had to add padding to help me swell up to about a fifty treble D cup. I also wore a tight Roman skirt and had a head of huge feathers. The Mazeppa character I was playing was supposed to be an overweight past-it stripper in a nightclub, so I was to flaunt any piece of belly fat I had out front. I had put on a little weight at the time, so when I stuck out my stomach, what I saw in the full-length dressingroom mirror was a figure that looked like a statue of Buddha on the bottom half and Big Chief Crazy Horse on the top. My very good friend and top actress Anna Manahan told me after opening night in the Gaiety that she screamed laughing when I hit the stage with my bra tassels twirling and my pushed-forward belly fat ponderously trying to keep up with the rhythm of the rasping 'You Gotta Get A Gimmick'. It was 'Be kind to outsized women' night, with a strong 'Fat is beautiful' theme. Nothing was held back, giving every lady in the audience over thirteen stones a great lift and a good belly laugh as well. I loved playing this part and enjoyed every minute of the run of *Gypsy*. As well as playing Mazeppa, I was understudying the lead part of Rose, excellently handled by Rosaleen Linehan, with whom I was to work later in her own play *Mary Makebelieve* at the Gate Theatre, and also in Seán O'Casey's *The Plough and the Stars* in the Gaiety.

Pantomime, probably more than anything else, helped to establish me as, how shall I put it, a woman for all seasons, a versatile artist, a 'character', and a credible force in showbusiness. It was a great shop window to display hitherto hidden talents. I've seen so many artists suddenly showing abilities that they didn't even know they had themselves. When you're working alone you get settled in what you are doing and it's more difficult to learn and progress. But when there are a lot of people working together, that brings out more in the individual, we push each other further, with no one wanting to be the weak link in the chain. Everyone learns from everyone else, and when you see someone whom you identify with say, singing, doing a handstand and tap dancing, you're inclined to think to yourself, 'I could do that.' From the time I was a child, I've always loved pantomime. I suppose like all young children, I thought everything was real and wanted to live in the wonderland where exciting things happened, where everyone was so happy, and where even the evil witches and monsters became good in the end.

When the curtain comes up on yet another pantomime, with all its over-the-top, over-obvious plots and conclusions, and glittering, colourful costumes, music, lights, singing, dancing and clowning, children and adults alike could never imagine the amount of hard graft, time and serious work that takes place beforehand. In the Gaiety, where I've worked in so many pantos, the people who start working earlier than anyone else, in fact months before rehearsals begin, are the wardrobe crew. These ladies make, stitch by stitch, every costume in the entire pantomime. Sadie Looney, who has been wardrobe mistress for more years than she cares to remember, following in the footsteps of her mother before her, despite thinking up fantastically colourful costumes year after year, never fails to pull out something extra-special to improve upon them the following year. The team which assists Sadie with all this work consists of Katherine 'Kay' Walton, Frances Boardman and Marie Clasby. Anyone who has ever seen the finale of any pantomime in the Gaiety Theatre will agree that these ladies have a wonderful talent.

Rehearsals for a panto start four weeks before the first preview, when all the cast meet in the dress circle at the Gaiety and the script is read. As we get the feel of the storyline and plots, suggestions are put forward and discussed until everyone is happy with that they are doing, no matter how long it takes. From producer Aileen Connor, director Mavis Ascott, musical director Andy O'Callaghan, band leader Earl Gill, dance captain Joyce Richardson, set designer Barbara Bradshaw, wardrobe, lighting, sound and stage crew, the standard of professionalism is always a pleasure to be part of and leaves nothing to be desired. Rehearsing six days a week from ten in the morning until six in the evening, not a moment is wasted. While Mavis would run certain dialogue for a scene with a small group, Joyce would work with the dance routines. In the beginning, miniature props and sets would be put at our disposal by Barbara, so we could get used to saying our lines while handling items and moving to appropriate positions in the particular scene. For a whole month it is a constant merry-go-round of learning lines and putting them into practice, running over songs and trying to keep up with sometimes torturous dance routines, a break for an hour, and then back on the merry-go-round. I think what a really good pantomime is all about is people. People on stage, back stage, front stage, the audience, children and adults alike, all needing one another to turn a show into a wonderful occasion. We have to thank people like Maureen Potter, Jimmy O'Dea, Jack Cruise, Danny Cummins, Cecil Sheridan, and a host of other wonderful artists who kept panto alive over the years for a new set of 'troupers' to take over. These troupers included the talents of Derek Chapman, Jacinta White, Nick Grennel, Rebecca Smyth, Joe Conlon, the hilarious Darrix brothers from Italy, a close relation of mine, Val Fitzpatrick, Gerry Walshe, and many more, all equal to the task.

To work with comedian Brendan Grace is an experience he doesn't let you forget. He's a notorious ad-libber and trickster, so you're never sure of what's coming next. He just believes in having fun all the time, with the result that even in a serious part of a scene, he might just come out with a funny remark under his breath and leave you struggling to stop laughing out loud and forgetting your lines.

By far the most professional artiste I've worked with was Adele King, better known as 'Twink'. When she was on stage her workrate was incredible, she stuck to the script, had a brilliant rapport with the audience and exuded the confidence that only real talent can. She is a great trouper, someone I admire very much, a friend and one of the best fellow artistes I have ever 'threaded the boards' with.

There is always a wealth of talent coming up through the ranks, and one such talent destined to grace the pantomime stage for years to come is June Rodgers. When she was picked to play an ugly sister in *Cinderella*, with me completing the cruel pantomime duo, I had never met her, although she was a successful comedienne around the cabaret venues. I was hoping she wouldn't have an 'attitude' or be awkward to work with, and I suppose she was thinking the same thing herself about me. June was a delight to work with, we 'jelled' from day one, and this considerably lightened the heavy workload of two performances a day, six days a week, for three weeks, with only Christmas Day off, and from then to the end of the panto, six nights a week with an extra show on Saturdays. Although the schedule is physically draining, there is no mental strain when people are compatible and look forward to working with each other.

Unfortunately my memories of pantomimes are not all happy ones. One in particular brings back such painful memories that I will spend as little time as possible describing its disastrously 'gory' details. It involved a partnership of myself, Alan Amsby, and a reluctant Sonny Knowles. Sonny, the darling of the 'sing-along' and a most charming man, said, and I quote, 'I was persuaded by Eileen in a moment of weakness to lend my name to this adventure, and afterwards literally prayed that it would end', unquote. Jimmy wrote the script and I directed the pantomime. I hired all the cast, the band, the props, and after 'setting up camp' beside my phone, booked it into dozens of halls around the country. When I couldn't find the phone numbers of potential venues, I used to ring up the police stations in large towns and ask them who was in charge of the local parochial halls and how could I contact them. After very stormy rehearsals incorporating problems and setbacks that I never dreamed could happen, and hiring a big luxury coach, with high hopes and loads of enthusiasm, we set out on our perilous Christmas tour. The name of the panto was *Jack and the Beanstalk*, and by the time it mercifully concluded, I could have done with some of the golden eggs at the top of the tree to settle bills, and even better, a few magic beans to swallow and perhaps make me disappear.

Some of the venues were well organised, the committees did their homework with regard to advertising and ticket sales, big crowds, came and the very well-received panto was asked about a return visit. Unfortunately these were few and far between, and barely served to keep our financial heads above water. I went through every emotional feeling a human being could possibly go through during this very good, wonderfully put together 'comedy of errors'. I was *angry* with people who didn't bother to put any work into advertising or promoting the show they had booked, and with the petty and childish complaints from some of the cast. I *cried* when the coach broke down and hundreds of children were disappointed at not getting their New Year's Eve treat, resulting in distress and a distasteful court case. I was *bewildered* when an audience of twelve people gave a standing ovation at the end of a pantomime that went ahead despite, due to partial power failure in the hall, being without sound or a band, with only a few bulbs lighting and our determination to fulfil our contract to keep us going. Fair play to the organiser, he paid the fee, and fair play to that great balladeer Christy Moore, who enthralled a couple of thousand people a few hundred yards away. I *laughed* when one of the three-feet-high boots that the panto's giant wore, broke in an offstage accident and he had to walk onto the stage, to spine-chilling music, standing no taller than I was, and then having to climb onto the outsized chair where he sat to 'terrify' everybody. I was *frightened* when a committee ordered 'heavies' to stop us and our equipment from leaving a hall after they had demanded monies that were not due to them, and *relieved* when, with the help of the police, whom I had called for assistance, we left in peace. Finally, I was *thankful* for the experience it gave me and *sorry*, but for a little more luck, it might have turned into a great success.

I was never a theatre-goer, not even to this day. I wasn't

'into' plays and wasn't drawn to cinema or the arts, whereas some of my colleagues in the entertainment business went to see everything presented in theatre. If I was asked to do a part in a play, I wouldn't read the play in question, I would just read my part and do it. This peculiarity of mine was applied when, against all the odds, I was given the role of Rosie Redmond in the 'mega' production of Seán O'Casey's *The Plough and the Stars* in the Gaiety Theatre. I had never read the Irish playwright's masterpiece and I wasn't going to. I only read Rosie Redmond's part, the rest didn't interest me. How I got this great cameo part is beyond me, looking at my course record, or rather lack of it, in the straight-acting field. Up until then I had never appeared in a straight-acting role, the little talent that I had being directed towards variety only. I was in panto at the Gaiety during the Christmas period of 1988 and heard about auditions taking place for parts in *The Plough and the Stars*. Everyone was discussing it, and this particular production of the O'Casey classic was the talking point of the theatre world. I remember asking Sadie Looney if she knew whether all the parts were gone, and she was pretty sure that the principal roles had been snapped up by the cream of Ireland's stage actors and actresses. She wasn't sure if the part of Rosie Redmond was cast so, on a whim, I made a bold 'never know your luck' phone call to the Gaiety School of Acting in Baggot Street.

The phone call was well worthwhile; 'no', the part was not cast, and 'yes, you may audition for it'. I thought 'Here we go again' as I recognised the bevy of really well-known actresses who turned up for the 'cattle call'. This time I thought I was completely out of my depth, I was fighting on foreign ground here, where Ethel Merman and the fairy godmother had no place. Nevertheless, I put my heart into the audition and was totally 'bowled over' when top director Joe Dowling gave me the go-ahead to play Rosie. I had never been so nervous as I was turning up at the first rehearsal for this 'state of the art' gig. When I met the cast I was in awe, standing among such Irish acting greats as Donal McCann, John Kavanagh, Rosaleen Linehan, Anita Reeves, David Herlihy, Catherine Byrne and Lorcan Cranitch. I never knew that Ronnie Drew and Paddy Moloney, of the world-famous ambassadors of Irish music, the Dubliners and the Chieftains, had offsprings in the acting field, until I met Phelim Drew, who played a soldier, and Aiden Moloney, who portrayed Mollser in the *Plough*. My pantomime friends from wardrobe, 'Kay' Walton and Frances Boardman, were familiar faces, as was Sadie Looney, who teamed up with the play's wardrobe designer, Consolata Boyle. Barbara Bradshaw was the scenic artist, and my old chum Gerry Lundberg looked after the publicity in his usual efficient way. I never realised what a really big production it was, and I wasn't relishing the thoughts of facing perfectionist Donal McCann in our high-charged emotional scenes together. I knew by what I had heard through the grapevine that the word going around was that Joe Dowling had flipped his lid employing a former showband singer to 'mix-it' with Ireland's acting élite. I didn't want to let Joe's trust in me down and was afraid that Donal McCann might say that he couldn't work with me, or I wasn't up to scratch. Donal was a perfectionist, a professional and an incredible actor, but he was also a gentleman, and after a tentative start we got on like a 'house on fire'. The rest of this highly talented cast were very nice people who treated me as one of the family and, judging by my complete lack of experience at this level, with great respect.

Rehearsals, which lasted a month, went very well, and as was expected, everyone knew what they were about very quickly and efficiently. I was getting along well, I knew my lines, where to be at any particular moment, and what to do during every second of the scene I was in, but something was missing. Even after we had done some dress rehearsals with costumes and make-up and hairstyles of the period, I just wasn't happy with the look or the characteristics of Rosie Redmond. Joe Dowling wasn't entirely satisfied with my overall look either, after trying different wigs and make-up and even suggesting I dye my hair red, which I didn't entertain at all. My appearance was left the best way we could think of right up to the first performance of the play at the opening preview. I was in my dressingroom getting myself ready for my straight-acting début, and when I'd finished putting on my make-up I kept looking in the mirror and thinking, 'This is not how she should look.' This woman was a weather-beaten prostitute who frequented bars and didn't really look after herself. I looked too healthy, too young, and had an air of respectability about me. I knew that I couldn't get 'into the part' and act it well if I didn't have a feel for what she really looked like and the way she carried herself. As I struggled with the problem, I suddenly thought of a woman I knew as a child, who was a prostitute and used to talk to men occasionally in our local park. Her face came back to me. She was past being attractive, and advancing age left lines under her eyes. The loss of interest in herself left knotted hair that hadn't been washed in weeks, lipstick a few days old, and make-up on top of yesterday's make-up. Her sense of confusion between being wanted and not wanted gave her a pitifully false air of well-being, which she flaunted through slurred speech after a few drinks. 'That's her,' I said, 'that's the Rosie Redmond I can identify with and the character that should be acted out in this play.'

I went to work on my face, making it drawn and pale, with dark circles under my eyes. I made my lips smaller and put on wine-coloured lipstick, which gave me a 'pinched' look, and then I back-combed my hair vigorously and pulled it back tight with a makeshift 'bun' at the rear. I had my hair looking flea-ridden, as if it hadn't been washed in years. When I was satisfied with the look, I said, 'She has to be half-jarred as well', and started doing my lines with slurred speech. When I had got the whole thing together I suddenly thought, 'What am I doing, I can't make all these changes without telling anyone, such a practice would be unheard of in the theatre.' After thinking for a minute I decided I would do it anyway, and besides, it was too late to tell anyone now and I just couldn't get into the part the way I was looking beforehand. Without getting permission from the director, I knew I was taking a big gamble, and if it didn't come off I surely would be booted out of the company.

David Herlihy was the first one I had serious dialogue with in the pub scene, and when he heard my opening lines he nearly forgot his. He told me afterwards that the only thing that came into his head when he saw and heard me was, 'My God, she's drunk.' Donal McCann was the next to have discourse with me, and although he knew he was looking at and listening to a different character than he had rehearsed with, he, true to form, didn't bat an eyelid and carried on as if we were doing the scene all our lives. This part of the play brought us into an interval, and I headed straight upstairs to my dressingroom. The rest of the cast, including Donal, were convinced I had hit the bottle and were probably glad my participation in the play was finished for that particular night. As a matter of fact, I thought my part had finished permanently, that I would be sacked and never work in the theatre again. I was the only one on the stairs and my heart nearly stopped when who comes down the steps towards me but Joe Dowling. He stopped, smiled, put out his hand for me to shake, and said, 'I never met her until tonight. Hello Rosie Redmond.'

The Cadets return

'*I*f the cap fits . . .' — and after all those years we wondered would they, as music agent Tony Byrne suggested to me that a comeback by the Cadets showband was a viable proposition in 1987. It wasn't just the cap, but every other measurement that was considered as the former Cadets' members said yes to Mr Byrne's proposal. Surprisingly, after twenty-five years the boys were not much heavier than they were in the sixties. We were blessed having Jas Fagan, our trombone player, as our personal tailor, to make exact replicas of the original uniforms. Jas had plenty of practice in his Thomas Street clothes shop making miniature Cadet uniforms for little boys making their Holy Communion, to the delight of their mammies who thought it a great idea.

The rehearsals were a bit of a nightmare, trying to find suitable times for busy husbands and now part-time musicians. Thanks to these numerous rehearsals and Jas's skilled hands, we sounded and were dressed exactly like we were in the sixties — we could only blame Father Time for the slight difference in our personal appearances. When we played in the Braemor Rooms cabaret lounge on Dublin's southside, our teenage children and nieces and nephews came along out of curiosity. The children didn't know what to expect, and when we were announced on stage some of them raced to the toilet in case they might be embarrassed with what they heard. The sixties' music was and still is very popular with the young, and our going on stage that night gave them a great blast from the past. The audience, including all the teenagers, had a great night, with our own kids dancing away, all very proud of their Mam and Dad at the end of the show.

The reformed Cadets had great fun reliving the past and touring for a few months, but as they say in professional boxing circles, 'they never come back', so like all smart boxers when they know it's time to stop, we 'hung up our gloves', despite the fact that gloves were the only part of the naval uniform we didn't have.

Part Four

Nothing compares to you

*I*t was the latter part of December 1990, another pantomime was in full swing, and during one of my rare visits to my mother in Patrick Street, I met Kitty, my sister, who by coincidence happened to be visiting at the same time. The conversation somehow got round to one of Kitty's more recent visits to a Marian shrine. Although I wasn't really interested in her religious activities, I did grasp that she had had a very interesting experience in Medjugorje, which she never discussed at length with me. She had no idea what state my life was in with regard to God, but she is the type of person who never lets a chance go by without giving 'the Almighty' a plug. This was one of the times when she did seize the opportunity of a divine commercial and asked me if I would like to accompany her to a three-hour service conducted by Father Aiden Carroll in University Church on St Stephen's Green. The only two words that really sunk in were 'three hours', which I repeated to Kitty with a look of disbelief on my face. I thought Kitty had definitely oversold the idea when she added that three Rosaries would be said besides the Mass, a homily and a blessing. 'Three full Rosaries? I'd eat them first,' I said with a negative resolute tone in my voice. This attitude didn't put Kitty off in the least, but what she didn't realise was that I hadn't been to Mass or Confession since 1976, and I had no intention of making this single trip back into a gruelling marathon. Kitty did say, 'When you get a chance', so this gave me till the middle of February, when the panto ended, to change my mind.

By the time my Gaiety Theatre Christmastime residency

had finished, Kitty's invitation had completely left my mind. Although the nights were now my own, I wouldn't have the after-show company, and this would leave an emptiness of sorts for somewhere to go between gigs or the next theatre show. I just didn't want to stay at home on my nights off, and after running out of ideas as to where to go on this particular night, I was so desperate to get out I would have gone to a bingo session. Then I remembered it was Wednesday, why not go to that church thing Kitty was talking about. It would be better than staying home and it would please Kitty no end. I had forgotten the name of the church and its whereabouts, so I rang Kitty. She told me where to go and advised me to be there before seven-thirty. When I arrived I thought I'd take a sort of observer's seat, comfortably near the back and preferably near an exit. Kitty had other ideas, as she 'horsed' me up to the very front, explaining that she and her friend Marjorie did a bit of singing during the service, and when the church got packed, I could hold their seats while they were chanting. When the whole thing started, I thought I'd just take stock, go through the motions, and then get out. It didn't happen that way.

I sat there like someone whose conscience was being examined. I was confused and totally out of touch, with an isolated feeling of having absolutely nothing in common physically or spiritually with the rest of the congregation. Everyone, row by row, went to receive Communion, except me. I just couldn't go, I hadn't been to Confession, I just wanted to get out. If I hadn't been so into myself, I would have got up and walked out. But I was worried about what people would think of me, maybe they would get the impression that I felt this sort of thing wasn't good enough for me. I was like a pagan, not knowing whether to sit or stand, and staying silent during all the strange new prayers. Catholic how are ye — I was carrying the name and nothing more.

As I began to try to think, some hard facts were coming

through to me. I realised that I had never ever mixed with the ordinary person in the street, my whole adult life was spent with entertainers and absorbed with the entertainment business. I never thought there was such a divide until I was sitting there among people who may as well have been from another planet. I had no time for 'ordinary Joes', we just couldn't communicate, they hadn't the power or influence to further my career, and so associating with them was a mere waste of time. I seemed to have the human race pidgeon-holed for my own convenience. At music-business receptions I looked out for the most important people, hoping they would notice me, wanting to be seen in their company and to hear them say that I looked well, all for the sole purpose of furthering my ambitions.

I slowly began to realise that literally everything I did in my life was self-centred, everything was planned with 'me' in mind. I didn't hear one word Father Carroll was saying — my conscience was running riot. For the first time in my professional career I began to think about the people around me. These people were not here to get something from anyone else, except God. They weren't using one another, as I saw it in my profession, but were coming to the real source of what life was all about. What a contrast to the merry-go-round I was on, looking on gigs, parts in plays, managers, booking agents, pub owners, as if they controlled my life and destiny, feeling bitter when failure came, and putting success down solely to my own hard work. I only wanted the big parts, the centre-stage, so I could be looked up to, and the more successful I was, the greater the bitterness when disappointment came. Looking out all the time, dressing to attract attention, men and compliments, I had neither the time nor the inclination to look inwards. I blamed everyone else when things went wrong, and got easily annoyed with 'fools' who didn't do it my way. If I seemed to have more talent, fame, or material things than these people, then I should be the one coming to God to thank him for his extra gifts. Instead, it was people like these, who seemed to have been given less, who were here praising God. I wasn't content with what I had been given, and didn't realise that I could be happy and at peace doing my thing with the gifts God gave me if only I acknowledged where they came from.

As I sat uncomfortably in the middle of all these strangers, who seemed to be in no doubt about the course of their lives and where they wanted to go when they died, I thought about little comments I had heard people make over the years. Statements like 'Ah! I'll just enjoy my life as I see it and live it as it comes to me, and when I'm old and grey, I'll probably get religious and confess to God before I die' or 'When I'm finished with this world, then it will be time for God', were among the many examples of bar-room wisdom I was accustomed to. Now, sitting in that church, I was living proof that this philosophy does not work. I just couldn't say I was sorry, when it was convenient, and really mean it. Here I was confronted with Him. I tried to look at the tabernacle but couldn't, because I didn't know what to say. I thought, what a turnabout, from the happiness and enjoyment I had felt at being in God's house when I was young, to the embarrassing trap I was in now. I was happy with God as a child, and God never changes. I felt because I was sitting there with no escape that I should be able to say 'I'm sorry', I was in the 'sorry' mode, but I couldn't feel anything when I said it. I was talking from my neck up. I even tried to pour it on, like an acting part, but that fell away — even an amateur actress like me knew it was a bad performance.

The whole service was a three-hour irritation that turned into downright suffering, and ironically Christ suffered for three hours on the Cross before his Father, and mine, took his Spirit. My mind was in turmoil. As the service came to a close, I couldn't wait to get out and assess the situation. Moving towards the exit, Kitty turned to me and said, 'Well! Did you enjoy that?' She obviously thought I had a ball. I said 'Oh yes', and after being quizzed by her as to whether I would go again, I concluded the conversation with 'I'll see'.

I eventually got into my car and, sitting there alone, thought, 'God, this is dreadful! Why, why, why did I feel that way? I shouldn't have felt like that.' The shocking reality of the seriousness of mortal sin and my deliberate indifference to God was brought home. I shuddered at the thought of dying suddenly, not being reconciled to God. I got home and explained to Jimmy how I felt in the church, and when he asked 'Are you going back?', I could have said no, but I didn't. The truth was, I did believe in God. I had felt ashamed and awful in the church only because I knew and believed Christ was truly present in front of me in the Eucharist. If I didn't believe that, I would never have felt this way. I believed in God but had never got to know him. I had never read the Gospels, the Bible was totally foreign to me, in fact I had only opened a Bible twice in my life, and on both occasions I happened to be staying over in a hotel with the Cadets. With nothing to read before going to sleep, I had taken up one of the Gideon Bibles and glanced through it. All the 'cometh's and 'thou goeth's sounded like that Shakespeare writing which I didn't like or understand, so I just left it down. I did know that Christ was born in a stable and that he rose from the dead, but I didn't know what he said to his Apostles, or that I was supposed to take up my cross every day and follow him. St Paul didn't ring a bell with me, all his letters were 'lost in the post'. I also knew about the Annunciation, but only the bare facts, not what it meant and its great importance to me. I only read magazines like *Cosmopolitan,* and even then I just looked at the pictures and read the captions. I was either too lazy or uninterested to delve into the lengthy articles under the captions. It was the same with the Word of God and the life of Christ, I just read the headlines and didn't go any deeper.

Because I couldn't understand why I was so distressed during my first visit to the church service, I just had to go back and investigate. This time I went to listen, and I was fully prepared to sit through the three Rosaries. I went to Confession beforehand, and because I was now more familiar with my surroundings, I reckoned I wouldn't stick out like a leg of lamb in a chemist's shop. I left my conscience alone and didn't feel too uncomfortable, despite the fact that I still didn't understand what the Readings or Gospel or homily were supposed to be telling me. All the people in the church appeared to be content with what they were hearing, and although I didn't even pass my Primary Certificate examination in school, I felt I should be intelligent enough to grasp what they seemed to understand.

Before my third weekly visit, Kitty introduced me to Father Aiden, who paid me the courtesy of knowing who I was. I took the opportunity of asking him if I could have a chat in private with him some time. His idea of privacy was walking around St Stephen's Green, but it turned out to be the best place, because anywhere you learn something beneficial is the best place. I poured my heart out while he listened wisely, commenting only occasionally, letting me get it all into the open.

After this, and before my fourth visit to the church, I told Jimmy I would have to get a Bible. Next day, Jimmy arrived home with a blue Bible which he said was on special offer. When I saw it in his hand I thought I would be wallowing in more 'Who I am's, 'tribes in the desert' and 'cometh and goeth's. I figured the best place to read this was sitting up in bed before I went to sleep. At 11 pm that night, hours before my normal time, I took the blue Bible to bed, and for some unknown reason I immediately decided to begin at the New Testament. What surprised me first was that there seemed to be hardly any New Testament, the greater part of the book was about everything else.

I was only a few pages into Matthew's Gospel when I started laughing, and when Jimmy asked what was so funny, I just said, 'This is all true.' 'I know it is,' he replied, as I continued reading. I was completely zapped. I knew the excitement, the euphoria that Edison must have felt when the bulb stayed lighting. Well, this bulb stayed on and not only gave light, but an eager hunger to know more. This was the truth, and nothing but the truth. It was as if Jesus jumped out of nowhere and, with that red book in his hand, surprised me with, 'Eileen Reid! This is your life', except that in this case it was a little blue book. I saw the truth in writing, it was so different from hearing it from somebody, and I thought, this truth was so important it had to be written down. I had never even read a novel in my life, but this book levelled me. I was reading it until five o'clock in the morning. The next few nights were the same, back to this fascinating book. The days were uninteresting, I just looked forward to learning, no, discovering, the new, no, the only way to live. This book had a huge effect on me, it was on fire, and I believed every word I read.

What I couldn't believe was the experience I was going through, because I had just opened this book as if I was opening a magazine or newspaper, just to see what I might find. What I found was a complete reversal of my terrible ordeal during my first visit to Father Aiden's service. Whereas one brought me right down, this one lifted me right up. I hasten to add that this is no reflection on Father Aiden, on the contrary, without the one I would not have discovered the other.

From what I had read and with my natural eagerness and impetuosity, I didn't hesitate to take Jesus up on his invitation to 'ask, seek and knock'. I must have sounded like I had lost my marbles, walking around the kitchen on my own, talking out loud to God about this and that, and particularly about the Holy Spirit whom he had sent to guide me. I asked the Holy Spirit straight out about Mass and Communion, because I had almost totally disregarded them for fifteen years. I knew the strict rule of the Church was, Mass once a week, Confession and Communion at least once a year. The answer came back immediately — if you ate once a year or even once a week, what state would your body be in? I wasn't concerned about the state of my body, so I put two and two together and knew right away that the food I was really looking for was to be found in the Mass, and this was what I needed in order to build up my spiritual life and get closer to this wonderful God whom I was desperate to know more about. The last time I was at Mass I hadn't a clue what was going on. It was through reading the Bible and asking the Holy Spirit that I learned everything about the Mass — how Jesus is present on the altar, how he is the priest and the victim, how he is truly present in the Eucharist, and when I receive this most precious gift of all, I am receiving the Child of Bethlehem and the Bread of Eternal Life.

I developed a hunger for the Mass, going twice a day, and even nine times one day, and enjoying every one. I took Jesus at his word, literally, and said, 'I'm going to annoy you now, with all I want to ask and look for and have opened.' I had been selfish with my life, now I was going to be selfish with God. I actually felt I could have a telephone conversation with someone, although not visible, but absolutely true to all his promises. I said 'Give me, give me', and he was delighted to give me. He loved me so much that I wanted to return his love, to do things for him, in fact I told him straight out that I wanted to do everything for him. This time I was answered with a question, 'Do you realise what you are saying, that you are prepared to give your will to me?' My response was simple — 'Is that all? Of course I'll give it, after all you've done for me, you needn't have asked.'

Little did this foolish woman know that she was shooting herself in the foot, and in the heart, because she had actually promised God that she would get rid of her old self totally. The trouble was, I couldn't see what God saw, all the barriers I had erected between us over the years, that would now have to be broken down if I was to keep my hasty promise. I couldn't see how I would have to be hurt in emptying myself of me to give myself to him. Taking stock of myself, I discovered that I was guilty of everything I found so annoying in others. What God tolerated in me, I couldn't tolerate in others. In finding fault with others, it was my attitude that was at fault. The list was piling up. Looking inwards, I discovered that I hadn't just a plank in my eye, but that both eyes were boarded up. 'Taste and see that the Lord is good.' Well! I had had a taste and it was good, but now I wondered would the taste of my neighbour be as palatable. Don't get me wrong, I never hated anyone, and over the years did innumerable charity gigs, some a little reluctantly, but the vast majority because I genuinely wanted to help. The truth is, I loved people from afar, the further away the better.

But Jesus is not only the most gentle, the most understanding and the most helpful, he is wisdom itself, and he knew that if I really wanted to stay close to him I would need to pray for his divine help, his graces, to overcome my human sinfulness. Still, knowing that you can't make a silk purse from a sow's ear, I was certain that making a caring person out of yours truly was going to tax even God's grace-bank.

The missing witness

*I*got to know Father Aiden Carroll pretty well over the next few months, so when he decided to organise a triduum, or three-day service, to commemorate the apparitions of our Blessed Lady in Medjugorje, I asked if I could help in any way. The services were to be held on consecutive nights in the National Stadium, the Mansion House, and in University Church. Although big crowds were expected, Father Aiden wanted to let people from outside the Dublin area know of the event, so a radio plug would be 'just what the doctor ordered'. Because I was not so much a 'pretty', but rather a 'familiar' face around the radio and television stations at Montrose, I thought I might be able to coax a plug for Father Aiden on the airwaves. So, armed with a few posters, I walked into the radio station and straight away met Julian Vignoles, a producer I had worked with before and a very pleasant person. He was accompanied by Joe Duffy, who is, for the benefit of Japanese readers, one of Ireland's top broadcasters, and a man I had never met before. When I asked him for the favour of a mention of Father Aiden's triduum on his programme, explaining that God never got a look in on radio or TV, I was surprised when Joe replied, 'You're right, he doesn't', and continued, 'What's it all about anyway?' I was merely explaining to him from the poster because I knew nothing in depth about Medjugorje, not having been there in person, and as I spoke Joe interrupted me and said, 'I'll go one better for you. I'll invite you onto my show if you're willing to come and talk about it.' He completely floored me with this, my heart dropped, and I got such a fright that I blurted out 'Oh no! I couldn't', but Joe put the boot in, saying, 'If you don't come on the show, forget about it.'

I was in bits leaving Montrose and headed off to see Father Aiden, rushing up to him and explaining what Joe Duffy had said. I pleaded, 'Will you do it, Father? I haven't got a clue what to say', but he simply told me to calm down and gave me a copy of Heather Parson's *A Light Between the Hills*, a book she had written about her experiences in Medjugorje. 'Go home and read it and you'll be fine,' he said.

Poor Jimmy was verbally attacked when I got home and he had to drop what he was doing to try to solve this problem for me. Methodically writing down on small plain postcards the main points explained in the book, Jimmy made up a handful of these little prompters to lead me through the bones of the story I was to explain on live radio. I complained that I couldn't pronounce the names of the Yugoslavian visionaries and that reading from the cards all the time would make everything sound ploddy.

On the day of the broadcast I was giving my daughter Pamela a lift into town and she put the precious cue cards and book into the glove compartment for safe keeping, despite the fact that I didn't want to leave them out of my sight. She complained that if we left them on the dashboard they would be sliding all over the place as we turned corners, so I let her put them away. 'You'll be OK,' were Jimmy's last words as he waved us goodbye, promising to have a listen in to the show at home.

After I dropped Pamela off in town, I took out my rosary beads and started to pray for guidance and help during my forthcoming radio interview. The only parking was quite a distance from the radio centre, and when I eventually got to the reception desk I gave the lady all the information she required. The girl in charge of the *Joe Duffy Show* was then paged, and when we exchanged greetings she said I had a few minutes to spare and would be welcome to a cup of coffee in the canteen.

When I entered the canteen it was empty, surprisingly, because there are always a few people there having a break. I got myself a cup of coffee and sat down, and on sitting down I suddenly realised I had neither book nor cards. I got such a fright that I stood up and almost knocked the coffee over, and right at that very moment, like a voice in my head, I heard 'Don't write anything down. What did Jesus say to his Apostles when he sent them out? "Remember it is not you who is speaking, it is me[the Holy Spirit]." ' As quickly as the terror had gripped me, it left me, and I sat down slowly and said, 'All right.' All my anxiety disappeared, it was as if I had been sedated, and I felt calm and full of peace. At that moment the girl in charge returned and asked if I was ready. I was led, I mean led, willingly and passively to talk on a live radio show about something I knew practically nothing about, and as Joe waved to me through his glass partition I hadn't a worry on my mind or a word on my lips.

I'm told we spoke for over fifteen minutes, and when we had finished, I had no idea what I had said. Joe exclaimed that it was terrific, and all connected with the programme were very pleased with the reaction through the huge number of phone calls relating to the broadcast. When I asked Jimmy what he thought of the interview he said, 'What interview? You did all the talking.' He said I sounded like an authority on Medjugorje and that he had taped it and would I like to hear the playback. 'No,' I said, 'I hate listening to myself', and left it at that. It would have been better if I had listened to the tape, because I didn't realise that I had been talking about my conversion. As far as I was concerned I was talking about Medjugorje on the programme, and Jimmy took it for granted that I knew what I had said, and that it was just a turn of phrase when I told him that I didn't remember anything about it. It wasn't until 3 April 1995, almost four years later, while we were writing this book, that it dawned on us that this Joe Duffy interview was my first witnessing to the power, love and mercy of God, and I was unaware of it happening. Before that interview I believed in, didn't question, and totally trusted the Holy Spirit, and knew that he would help me remember all I was supposed to know, all I had written down about the subject I was to discuss. When Jesus said, 'It is not you who is speaking', I didn't realise that he was also saying, 'It is not you who is choosing the subject on which to speak.' Both Jimmy and I had missed the whole significance of what had happened. Naturally poor Father Aiden thought that I knew I had actually witnessed to God on radio and he asked innocently if I would just say a few words about my coming back to God in the National Stadium and the Mansion House during the forthcoming triduum. I refused point blank, thinking I wasn't ready for this sort of thing yet, and gave him a friendly warning not to call on me on either of the nights. I was so afraid that I threatened never to come to any of his services again — not that he would be 'any the worse' for it — if he didn't promise not to call on me. He kept his promise and I was allowed to enjoy these nights of prayer and witnessing.

A painful decision

On reflecting back on my not-too-distant past, I can now identify very personally with some major issues in the news today. Different people have equally differing opinions as to which way laws may be changed, and how what they see as their needs can be accommodated. One of the main moral issues of today is abortion, the right to choose, the right to obtain information on abortion, which involves all sorts of complicated exceptions to Church and/or State laws. I thank God that I can not only publicly give my opinion on such matters, but also add my personal experience. I have no doubt whatsoever who is in control of life. God and God alone controls life. As I explained already, I was in the position that anyone who wants to have an abortion finds themselves in. At the time, I was desperate, I felt no one could help me. I wanted to keep the baby, but because of the circumstances, doing so would threaten my marriage. Although I wasn't a practising Catholic, I put my trust completely in God. He was my last hope, so I gave this terrible problem over to him. When I pleaded with him, I didn't say I'd be good from then on, or that I wouldn't do it again, but I did tell him that no matter what his decision was, I would accept it, no matter what it would cost me. I trusted that he would do the best thing for me. I wasn't going to have an abortion even if it meant being thrown out of the house by Jimmy, and I told God that. God answered me by taking the baby, and this was his will. I refuse to allow anyone to tell me that I had a miscarriage because of this or that, or anything I did to myself — it just isn't true. My local doctor and the hospital said there was no medical reason for it, I was a perfectly healthy woman. Even though Jesus knew I would walk away, a satisfied spoiled brat, like one of the nine lepers, and would continue doing my thing, he kept loving me, and still does today. If he had answered my plea by allowing the baby to be born, I would still have come forward to denounce abortion.

A couple of years ago I attended a small prayer group called the Shield Retreat, whose members came together to help each other to grasp the true meaning of the scriptures by calling on the Holy Spirit for guidance. On one of my thirteen weekly visits to this retreat, I was given a number of passages from the scriptures to study, one of these being the Annunciation. I prayed to the Holy Spirit for enlightenment on this mystery for two days, and on the morning of the third day, this is what came to me. God took Mary, a virgin, and put life within her. There was no man involved. He also took Elizabeth, Mary's cousin, who was well married, having intercourse with her husband for years, trying to have a family with no results. Although Elizabeth was advancing in years and was barren, she became pregnant. God had put life where a man couldn't. This brought it home to me that in every case it is God who controls life, no matter what the circumstances. No one has the right, or was given the right, to take life away. These children are not ours to do away with, they are God's other sons and daughters, his children. The womb is not just a receptacle, it is sacred, for God allowed his Son to be born from it. The womb is supposed to be a safe place, a holy place, it was Christ's first tabernacle. He could have come to us by any means, but he chose a woman's womb. What an honour he gave to women, the honour to bring, not theirs, but God's children into the world. We really are born of God, and he alone can demonstrate at any time or with anyone he chooses that this is true, by putting or not putting life where he wills. I'm not pointing a finger at anyone, for who am I to criticise or condemn, to pick up stones. I am simply telling it as I know

217

it and have experienced it, and my bottom line is that Christ is all loving, all merciful and all forgiving. Even if you have had an abortion, go back to him, open your heart to him, and you'll see what I mean. Don't try to justify it, return to him in Confession and he will wipe everything away. Never think it can't be forgiven, it's the time of great mercy. God will heal all your hurts and no one will accuse you. We are all sinners, and that's why he came to us, to save us. We all must carry our crosses, but he will lighten them if we just trust in him. I would love to think that I could help any girl contemplating abortion, who is frightened, not knowing where to turn, afraid of what others might think. I would be glad to sit down and talk. Abortion might seem to bring temporary relief, but it's not the answer, there is no happiness at the end of it. In my own case it would have been a selfish act, a convenient way of solving a problem that was disturbing my lifestyle. When the crunch point comes, it is not a vote for or against abortion, it's a vote for or against Christ. If we ignore God now, he will ignore us when we face him. As Jesus said, 'Whatever mercy you show, it will be shown to you.' If you are thinking of having an abortion, all I can say is — Don't Do It!

A very special friend

*I*n August 1991, Jimmy and I were invited, with Fr Aiden Carroll as spiritual director, to go to Medjugorje, a Marian shrine in Yugoslavia. I had never been there before, and as a matter of fact neither Jimmy nor I had ever been to a Marian shrine. I have to say at this stage that I am not and never was obsessed with the inclination or curiosity to go chasing off to be where any strange sightings or religious phenomena had been reported. I was going to Medjugorje for the sole purpose of honouring the Mother of God, praying, and enjoying the trip.

About two weeks before we went, I had a most wonderful and deeply emotional experience while I was in my back garden, of all places. I could not possibly do justice to this marvellous happening by trying to describe it in these pages, but in consequence of it I developed, among other things, a much deeper love and devotion to Our Blessed Lady. From just making a simple wish from the heart and invoking the name of the Mother of God, I had been privileged with this very moving experience, and I knew then I had to get to know her better. What better way to do this than by means of the Holy Spirit. A lot of Christians have a problem with Mary, but then again, up until this experience I had no particular devotion to her either. I could see now that God the Father gave us Jesus through Mary. I felt that in order to be closer to Jesus in every way, I would go to him by a simpler, softer, safer, surer way, so I consecrated myself and everything connected with me — my career, my home, my marriage, my family, all I have or ever will have — to Jesus through the

Immaculate Heart of Mary. When the archangel Gabriel said to Mary 'Hail, full of grace', God gave us an example of what state we should be in to receive the truly present body of Christ in the Eucharist. I feel we owe Mary so much, she is very, very important, for our salvation began with her saying 'Yes'. All the prophets throughout the ages were men, but God exalted a woman above them all when he sent his son to us and made Mary the Mother of Jesus, the Mother of the Church, and the spiritual mother of us all. Reading the Gospels, I saw that when Mary asked Jesus to help at the wedding feast of Cana, he said his time hadn't come yet, but he did help because his mother asked him. His whole ministry was brought forward because she asked for a simple human need. I can see now that Mary is interceding for us with Jesus, asking him, not to turn water into wine, but cold hearts into hearts filled with his love. Mary is now allowed to intervene, to help her other children, when she wasn't allowed to as her child Jesus died. In contrast to the wedding feast at Cana, Mary at this moment in time is coming to us to ask us, to plead with us, for conversions, complete change of hearts, and to embrace the peace and love of God. She points always to the only way we can find this peace and love — Jesus Christ, so I wonder is Christ prolonging his second coming for his mother's sake.

With so much happening to me spiritually, so much to understand and learn, I felt I had to get myself a spiritual director. From the discalced Carmelite Order attached to St Teresa's Church in Clarendon Street, the very patient, prudent Father Herman Doolan took on the task of helping me to understand the ways of the Lord, while keeping my feet firmly on the ground. I am now eating my words as far as the Rosary is concerned. I told Kitty that I would eat them first, now I'm saying three Rosaries a day. I consider the beads as the umbilical cord that attaches me to Mary, my Mother, just as Jesus was. It's the lifeline, the miniature life of Christ, and that life flows into me. Everything I do now, down to the simple things like cleaning the table, sweeping the floor and washing the dishes, my work on stage, everyone I work with on and off stage, in fact my every breath and heartbeat, I offer to God. Those who laugh at the idea of the Blessed Virgin coming to visit and warn us will be the very ones who will thank her for getting them the extra time. God spoke to the prophets, then he sent his Son, then he sent his Spirit, now he sends his Mother.

A place very close to my heart is the Marian Shrine at Knock, County Mayo, in the west of Ireland. I go there two or three times a year with Jimmy, who also has a great devotion to the Mother of God. It was shortly after I had returned from my first visit to Knock in May 1992 that I got a strong feeling that I was to organise a church devotion to Jesus and honour him through the prayers and intercession of the Immaculate Heart of Mary. I didn't know anything about what it would entail, what format it would take, or whether it would be on a weekly or monthly basis. I dismissed the idea, thinking that if it was just a whim it would not come back into my mind again. The idea kept coming back, however, so in order to get some advice on such a venture I decided to phone Father John Power, a wonderful Augustinian priest from Wexford, whom I had the pleasure of befriending while we were both in Knock the previous May, when he led a pilgrimage from Dublin. Father Power was extremely helpful, giving me some sound advice mixed with caution and encouragement. He told me that if the devotion was not prompted by a real spirit of prayerful commitment, it would fall away like so many others, but if it came from God it would last. He cautioned me about having a weekly devotion, because it might be difficult to get a different priest every week, and suggested that a monthly devotion might be more realistic. I said I didn't want to start this if Our Lady didn't desire it, but if she did, she herself would supply the priests. Fr Power not only gave the idea his blessing, but also promised to be the celebrant himself on some of the nights of this devotion, a promise he was to keep over the coming three years.

Because of a change in management at the Gaiety Theatre, I wasn't informed about my inclusion in the pantomime until August of 1992, when the preparations for the devotion were well under way. Thousands of publicity leaflets were printed and distributed giving all the details of its commencement, and the services of priests were booked for the following two months, as the first of the weekly Monday nights of prayer started in St Teresa's Carmelite Church in Clarendon Street. The more lengthy name I had thought up for the devotion was shortened to 'To Jesus through Mary' by Father Michael Maher, a larger-than-life character and Marist priest teaching in Chanel College, Coolock, in the suburbs of Dublin, who was to be the very first celebrant in Saint Teresa's on 28 September 1992.

Although I was happy that the devotion was 'up and running', I was a little uneasy about the prospect of being absent from Saint Teresa's for the two and a half month period of Monday nights while I was performing in the Gaiety. Our Lady knew that the panto was my bread and butter, but she also knew that, although I didn't start the devotion for myself, I would have to be at the church every Monday. I left the whole thing in her hands, and if ever I needed a sign that I was to continue the devotion, I got it when the following occurred. The pantomime, like all others in the history of the Gaiety, ran from Monday to Saturday inclusive, with Sunday night free. As we prepared for our customary four weeks of rehearsal, Aileen Connors, the producer, called me into her office to inform me of a different format the theatre was trying for the first time in its history. She explained that the free night would be changed to Monday, and there would be a Sunday afternoon show instead. I was absolutely 'floored' hearing this, and I knew leaving Aileen's office that day that I couldn't get a better sign that Our Lady was running the devotion. This new format at the Gaiety was a success and is continuing to the present day. After a year in Saint Teresa's, Clarendon Street, the devotion continued in Whitefriars' Carmelite church in

Aungier Street, still on Monday nights, except Bank Holidays, commencing at 7.15 pm with Mass, Rosary and Benediction, and finishing about 8.30 pm. I cannot thank the prior Fr Farragher and the priests of this really beautiful church enough for keeping it open and at our disposal for a devotion that has brought many great blessings to all who attend. As regards getting different priests each week, I had no problems at all — Mary just seemed to have the ones I phoned in the palms of her hands, because they always said yes and always came back again.

Through the devotion and through contacting priests, I had the pleasure of meeting Father Kevin Scallan and Sister Briege McKenna, whose work of spiritually helping, advising and encouraging priests takes them all over the world. Sister Briege of the order of Poor Clares is blessed with the healing ministry and is popularly known as 'the healing nun', although through her obvious love for Christ in the Eucharist she constantly informs all and sundry in no uncertain manner where the healing really comes from. Father Kevin had no second thoughts about helping out at the devotion on Monday nights, and still does so when he's home in Ireland. I just have to say that I am most grateful to them both for their friendship and for giving me encouragement and help with all the same sincerity and enthusiasm with which they joyfully spread the Word of God.

Till death do us part

Apart from being confronted with the terrible decision of whether to have an abortion or not, I also went through the trauma of falling out of love with my husband, and was facing the prospect of leaving him for good. This brings me, with the experience of knowing what I am talking about, to the subject of marriage, and all its trials and tribulations. It goes without saying that marriage is not working out for an awful lot of people today. Divorce is rampant in any country that allows it. The fact of the matter is, a marriage won't find the strength to last unless God is a real part of it. It's very simple — nothing that God is part of can collapse.

Now, through personal experience, I know that God would not put me in a situation, knowing all the difficulties I would have to face, without offering me the help and support I would need to make it work. It doesn't take a brilliant mind to realise that the family is one of the most attacked elements of society today, having such formidable enemies as financial pressures, unemployment, drugs and alcohol abuse, child abuse, infidelity, contraception, abortion, divorce, to name but a few. There is some hope for a family if the parents stay together, but divorce divides, and division is the last thing a family needs. In my case, as in so many others, I was faced with the realisation that I didn't want to go on with my marriage. I had 'gone off' Jimmy totally and was in the same position as any woman who wants to get away from her husband. I didn't want to be near him and would have disappeared from his life but for the children. I was offered a change of address by another man, and an invitation to bring the kids as well, but a number of considerations stopped me from taking up the offer, and Jimmy didn't figure in any of these. If anyone had told me then that I could fall back in love with my husband, I would have said, 'No way, it just couldn't happen.' He wasn't where my mind and heart were at, and I didn't want to be part of where he was at. This situation was going on for far too long to change.

Well, it did happen, everything was turned upside down, and I'm more in love with Jimmy now than I ever was before. Indeed, our love for each other is stronger now than when we first fell in love. No, Jimmy didn't win the National Lottery, it was I who won something far greater — the gift from God to recognise and believe that if I let him run things he'd give me everything I need to be genuinely happy.

Before I got to know Christ, I didn't look on sin for what it was, I didn't recognise it as sin, it was an acceptable and normal part of life. The Lord taught me to cut the bad parts from my life by following his teachings, and the difference this made to me was incredible. I didn't have to give up anything except the things that were causing me and those closest to me pain. I didn't have to go around in sackcloth and ashes with a long face. I remained as extrovert as I ever was and found myself getting much more enjoyment from life. Anyone who says God is boring is very wrong. He wants us to be happy. We can still have our sports, hobbies and careers and he will bless them and us if only we give him some of our time.

When I was asked to write this book, I knew God was giving me a wonderful opportunity to thank him and tell others. 'Speak now or forever hold your peace' is a familiar phrase, and how many times have we heard 'Would you put that in writing', so in living witness to the truth that God does care, I am speaking now and I am putting it in writing.

Nobody told me about Christ's healing love, nobody told me that a miracle could happen in my home and in my marriage, nobody told me that I didn't have to abandon my marriage vows when serious trouble appeared, nobody told me that there was a powerful alternative to making the selfish, hasty, wrong decisions that would only serve to deepen the wounds that could so easily be healed. I have experienced how seemingly dreadful situations can be reversed, and all I wish to anyone whose marriage is weakening or broken, is that they may open themselves to the same loving, understanding God that repaired mine. Making my own decision to leave Jimmy for whatever reason and going to live with another man would have meant living in mortal sin, and also contributing to my new partner committing mortal sin. I would then be living a lie if I went to Mass, saying I believed in God, then going off to do whatever suited me, leaving my so-called Christianity behind me in the church. Leaving my husband just because I didn't want to be with him any more surely wasn't what God had in mind when he joined the two of us to become one, to live through good times and bad, in sickness and in health, till death parted us. I liked the good times and the health, it was the bad times and the sickness that bothered me. Bad times were when things didn't go the way I wanted them to, and I never realised that sickness, apart from including such horrors as alcoholism, drug and gambling addiction and domestic violence, also included infidelity. When this latter sickness hit me, I thought that nobody could have a worse problem than mine, that my situation was different, more difficult, more ongoing, too hurtful to talk about to anyone, and just about impossible to solve. These same thoughts go through the minds of so many troubled people today, but the good thing is that although the situations may vary in seriousness, they all have one thing in common — their solution. Coping with and curing 'impossible' problems can become a reality if they are brought to the only one who can cure when all else fails, and the only one who deals in the impossible.

If Jimmy had not forgiven me, and instead abandoned

me, both he and I would have lost out on something wonderful, the happiness we now have, with both, and I repeat, both of us knowing where this happiness came from. Splitting up would also have had repercussions for the children, leaving scars, together with the possibility that both of us might live in unions outside the teachings, the laws and the blessings of Christ our Lord. I can clearly see now that love always overcomes evil, that God is love, that he must be loved first, following what he said about us not being worthy of him if we love someone more than him.

Against all odds

*T*he 1990s introduced me to a side of entertainment that I thought had definitely passed me by. The film industry thankfully caters for people of all ages, shapes and sizes, which is just as well, because my days of parading on a beach in a bikini are long gone. A chance meeting with film casting agents, Ross and her husband John Hubbard, in the Green Room at the Gaiety Theatre in 1990, turned out to be a very fruitful encounter. Ross is a real straight-talking, no-nonsense bubbly lady, who makes you feel very relaxed in her company, as she does in her home, where a party is a party and she proves she is the 'hostess with the mostest'. I was informed by Ross that auditions were taking place for parts in a major movie to be made in Dublin. The film parts involved Dublin characters and she thought it worth my while to try my luck.

I took Ross Hubbard's advice, auditioned for this upcoming movie, and landed the part of Mrs Quirk in *The Commitments,* directed by Alan Parker. It's a small world, I thought, as I met blonde and beautiful Angeline Ball, with whom I had worked in panto, and who was to play Imelda Quirk, my daughter, in the film. The Archbishop Byrne Hall off Harrington Street on Dublin's southside, not too far from my former home, was the location for the dancehall scene, and this was very familiar territory for me, having rehearsed pantomimes there.

During this very enjoyable first-time close encounter with the making of a movie, I was immediately struck by the amazing patience a movie director has to have, dealing with so many different personalities, hour after hour doing and redoing scenes, while trying to meet a deadline. Alan Parker was all things to all men and women on the set. He was a motivator, a father figure and a friend, so the work was completed with a mixture of efficiency, urgency and patience. The Olympic Ballroom, situated close by in Pleasant Street, where I used to listen to the Melochords on those Tuesday nights in the late 1950s, was used by the caterers, who fed everyone connected with the movie to bursting point. I looked and felt like somebody else as I sat waiting for my maiden appearance in front of the big screen cameras, dressed in middle-aged, settled-looking, very plain clothes, with no make-up and minus my customary curls.

Shortly after this first little taste of movie-making, and because of my newfound relationship with God, my attitude towards everyone and everything changed for the better. Auditions and their outcome, getting or not getting parts, people's behaviour towards me, and mine towards them, took on a whole new meaning. I wasn't anxious any more, I was genuinely pleased to see others being successful, and any resentfulness or jealousy I had took a back seat. I wasn't putting unnecessary pressure on myself anymore, whether I was successful or not. I trusted in God, accepted his will and knew that he had a reason for everything he allowed to happen.

There was certainly a reason why British television director James Hawe didn't bring a script with him as he auditioned me for a part in a BBC TV film called *Against All Odds*. As we sat in the Mont Clare Hotel in Clare Street, near Dublin's Merrion Square, he suddenly asked me to do an impromptu sketch, with him just ad-libbing as we went along. Without giving me a word of script, he asked me to act the part of an irate customer who confronts her bank manager having learned that the bank has bounced a very important cheque of hers, leaving her in a most embarrassing predicament. Both the director and his assistant laughed as I ranted and raved at my imaginary bank manager, and were so impressed that I got a 'meaty' little part in *Against All Odds*, a part that had me working in Dublin and Cork for ten days. This episode taught me to be always ready for the element of surprise, which is never far away in showbusiness. This is so true that I never know what to expect when my agent Teri Hayden, who heads 'The Agency', rings me. I am very happy to be associated with Teri, whose youth and petiteness belie her strength and experience in this hard-bargaining world of professional entertainment.

Renewing old friendships and meeting some famous people is a pleasant side to getting a part, no matter how small, in a film. In *A Man of No Importance,* which was directed by a very quiet gentleman called Sumi Krishnamana and starred Albert Finney and Brenda Fricker, I met up with an old friend, Joan O'Hara, with whom I had the pleasure of working in the comedy play *Nunsense* some years earlier. Mr Krishnamana knew I grew up in the heart of Dublin and appreciated all the help I could give him with regard to the fashions and hairstyles and customs of the 1960s period in which the film was set. He was very interested in the photographs I had of my beehive hairstyle of the sixties and asked would I sport that style in the part I had in the movie. I had to go to an expert in the form of Gary Kavanagh of Peter Marks' hair salon in Dublin, who did a fantastic job with a wig, matching my blonde colour perfectly and building the curls up just like in the old days. Despite the fact that the film was shot in the freezing temperature of February, and most of the time outdoors, on or about a bus parked along the quayside in Dublin, I have very fond memories of it.

I made a good friend in Anna Manahan, a gifted Irish actress and a great wit. I'll never forget how considerate, charming and down to earth Albert Finney was, how patient the director was, how diplomatic Anna Manahan was, and how freezing cold we all were. I have to laugh when I think of myself sitting on this bus dressed in a leopardskin coat, large rimmed glasses, small dog on my lap, and a handbag that never left my arm throughout the entire film. Even while they were filming outside, myself, Anna, Joan and others had to stay in the bus, and on a couple of occasions when the crew outside took a break, they totally forgot about us poor, cold, hungry creatures still sitting waiting for something to happen. For hour after hour we were like toy soldiers in a toy bus with hyperthermia setting in and the Jack Russell's patience running out. I was beginning to think that the good Lord had lavished everyone on the bus with an abundance of resilience, patience and dignity, when Anna Manahan, God bless her, led the revolt. Her few eloquent words certainly brought results, with no lesser a person than Albert Finney himself bringing hot food to lift the siege and indeed the hearts of these perishing passengers.

If I had any pride or vanity left in me it was exorcised when my next little movie part transported me from a bus with a dog to a jail with smallpox. When Oscar-winning make-up artist Michelle Burke, on the set of *Moll Flanders*, on location in Dublin Castle, was finished with me, I would have emptied any bus, freezing or otherwise, with my death-rattle cough and oozing sores. The scene I was in during this sorry eighteenth-century tale concentrated on a dark, rat-infested dungeon where, among other sordid happenings, I was dying of a dreaded disease. The biggest problem the director of *Moll Flanders*, Mr Pen Densham, had with my make-up was that no matter how old or sick-looking it made me, my bright blue eyes kept shining through. My hands were like boiling porridge, my hair like dirty straw, and my face full of sores, but my eyes still popped up full of life. Coloured contact lenses were the answer, leaving one of my eyes bloodshot and the other dim and uninterested. I only got one day's work with this film, but I suppose it's long enough to spend in jail with smallpox.

These little film parts were only a small portion of the things I found myself doing that I thought I would never do.

Things were happening for me that I thought would never happen, like when top director Michael Scott asked me to play the part of Mrs Lovett in the hit-musical *Sweeney Todd*, which ran at the National Concert Hall in Dublin in November 1994. I was more contented and relaxed than I had ever dreamed possible. My career had taken an upsurge while at the same time rivalry and competition had disappeared and teamwork and an atmosphere of peace had taken over. It wasn't important to me anymore whether I was successful or not, I was working for Christ now, not for myself, so my trust was in him and I went where he led me and tried to do what he wanted me to do.

I never thought that at fifty-two years of age I would be singing in pubs to young people in their twenties, and even those in their teens, and be part of the overall enjoyment of a 'night out'. I love to see people enjoying themselves, but through the 'eye' of the stage I can see more, having a deeper knowledge of those I entertain. I can see in front of me the young and the not so young, all sharing the differ-ence between enjoying a few drinks and alcohol abuse, and also sharing the experiences of celebration, consolation, hallucination and devastation that this potential curse can induce. I took the 'pledge' in 1991 and am now a pioneer for life because of past experience.

Over to the experts

*I*t may not be common practice for an author to hand over her pen and allow someone else to finish her book, but then I'm an unorthodox person, as you will probably have noticed. I know the readers will be wondering how Jimmy and the children felt about their unusual home life, so I thought the best thing to do was to give them the freedom to express in their very own words, albeit briefly, what they thought of life at home, me, and my shortcomings. At the time of writing, Pamela, Dermot and Claudine are single and still living at home. Pamela, who is twenty-six years old, works for a computer company, Dermot is a supervisor and is twenty-five years old, and twenty-two-year-old Claudine is a gym instructor.

Pamela

The one word that would describe my mother is 'different', but we were well looked after and loved. I wouldn't say home life was particularly happy or unhappy. I was happy as a child and frustrated as a teenager. I found my mother unapproachable, someone who was too wrapped up in her own world to understand any of the teenage feelings, insecurities and problems I may have had. I also felt very bitter about the lack of respect she had for my father and his happiness. I wasn't aware that there were extra-marital affairs earlier on but I do remember certain things, like seeing her parked at the top of the road in the car fixing her lipstick before she drove down to the house, and on other occasions whispering on the telephone. I remember her telling me when I was about fifteen years old that there had

been a problem in her marriage because of another man. I
don't know who was supposed to benefit from this useless
piece of information as she didn't seem very remorseful
while saying it, and only ended up pushing me further away.
Home life is much happier now and it's great to see Mam
and Dad more in love than a pair of newly-weds, as my dad
often says 'the darkest moment is before the dawn'. I'm just
glad to see that the sun shone through for them.

I consider religion to be a very private and individual
thing, but for myself it's a comfort to know that there's
always someone watching over me. I don't have any objections at all about this book being written, I trust Mam and
Dad's judgement and if it's right for them it's good enough
for me.

I was standing in the kitchen when Mam had her 'back-
garden experience' so I had a bird's-eye view of the whole
thing. Mam is a very open and honest person and would
have nothing to gain by fabricating such an event. I do
believe what she saw and I do believe God's love has touched
her in a very special way.

Dermot

It was strange when Mam turned up to collect me at school
wearing a bodysuit when all the other mammies had frocks
and scarfs on. She always told us not to care about what
other people thought or said and I didn't and still don't.
During my early life, say between eight years old and fifteen,
it was always my father rather than my mother that the
happiness was built around. My father always supported me
in everything I did and I will never forget this. The extra-
marital affairs did bring a not-too-happy atmosphere into
our home. When the family was together, I remember we
children would argue with Mam, especially Pamela. Our
home now is a hundred times better. We are all at ease in the
knowledge that our parents came through all that sh..t and
still love each other.

It taught me never to give up. God plays a huge part in my life. He was there when I needed him most and now I know he always will be.

I'm very glad Mam wrote this book, she needed it all to be known to clear her mind and soul. Mam is very genuine about her love for God and it shows by the amount of time she gives him. All during my life my father has been the reason behind my laid-back approach to life, my humour, my lack of any great interest in material things, and I hope if I am faced with what he has been through, that I will have the heart and strength to still love my family. Most important of all, he has taught me that no matter what happens, if you forgive people for what they do to you, you'll get on a lot easier in life. Nothing lasts forever, and all things will pass, so I think it's best to get on with life and make the most of it. God is there to help all of us, and my family is living proof of this. When we're in trouble, all we have to do is ask him to help. You don't have to be a boring old recluse or be praying all day to love God, but it's good to tell him you know he's there and give him some of your time.

Claudine

Although I knew my mam loved us dearly, she never seemed to have the time to be with us, partly because I felt that she had more important things to do. I don't recall any arguments between my mam and dad, probably because I was too young to remember. What I can remember is that my dad was extremely patient with my mother and even during the times when she would annoy everybody in the house to the point of us leaving, my dad was always there, loving and standing by her no matter what. I can't remember anything about the partying phase my mother was going through and I think it's best that way. What's in the past can stay there, I'm only concerned with here and now. I can't say that Mam is home more often now than she was back then, but now she's in church when she's not at home and that's much better than having her come home with shopping bags full of Brown Thomas' clothes that she doesn't need. She still doesn't make dinner, but the odd Sunday she might cook a few vegetables and potatoes.

I still don't discuss my feelings with my mam and I wouldn't be inclined to sit down with her and talk about how my day went. I'm just so used to not having my mother there to talk to that I have got into the habit of trying to solve my own problems. I know my mam would help me if I ever needed her, and I know how much she loves us, but we're not as close as I'd like us to be. My mam and dad's relationship together has blossomed again, and although my dad never stopped loving her, my mam loves my dad more than ever now. Mam no longer has the urge to spend fortunes on material things, and realises now how selfish she has been in the past. I realise of course that part of the reason she couldn't be with us more when we were younger was because she was gigging with a band and I don't blame her for that.

God means more than life to me and I love him more than anyone or anything in this world. Without him I am nothing and I thank him every day for what he has given me. I also thank him for bringing the love back into our house and for opening up my mother's eyes and for bringing her closer to my dad. I try not to miss Mass on Sunday and I pray by myself, but not enough.

I have no objections to this book being written, I'm thrilled that my dad's writing abilities have been finally put to paper. I believe that in the book the truth will offend some people, make others laugh, and some may cry, but it is the truth and it was with Mam's open consent when asked that it was written. I know my mam has changed now and no matter what may be written in the book about her past, whether it's good or bad, I'll still love her as much as I always have. We've all made mistakes in our lives and I'm proud that my mam had the guts to admit hers.

Jimmy

I would rather forget the painful memories that parts of this book bring back, and surely this is what I should be doing, as forgetting goes hand in glove with forgiving. But having said that, I can also say that forgiving is an extension of giving, and giving is the reason I backed the idea of the book and, in particular, its main theme. I wanted to give back to God some of the love he gave to me in such a miraculous way, and this book was the perfect opportunity that I couldn't miss. I know I will be asked many questions about my opinions of it, and my part in it, questions like, 'Why did I have to parade my private life in public, possibly causing embarrassment to my family, and why support the comments made on controversial moral issues that could even cause a rift with friends and family alike?' My answer to these two questions could be summed up in one word — gratitude, yes, gratitude to God for giving me a new life, for transporting me from a half-living state of doubt, unease and mistrust, into a full, happy life of peace, trust and real love. Those readers who have had or are experiencing unfaithfulness in their marriages already know its terrible effects, but to those who have been blessed with a lasting happy marriage, I would like to say, 'You have been spared a terrible trauma, just cherish and appreciate what God has given you, and don't ever forget to thank him.' What does it matter about embarrassment or rifts or resentment? I want to say to others who are suffering, 'If God can do wonders for me, he can do them for you as well.' Jesus gave me far too precious a gift to keep to myself, I just have to share it openly.

Another possible question might be — 'When did I find God and did I pray for Eileen during the bad times?' Well, I always believed in God and I did pray during the bad times, after all I was a Catholic, I went to Mass every Sunday and tried to keep the rules, but right there lay the real root of our problems. My paying lip-service to God was just not enough. As your average Catholic I was fulfilling obligations, I wasn't really praying, I wasn't open to him, I hadn't a clue how to love God and, more importantly, I had no idea how much God really loved me. So because of my weakness of faith, God couldn't use me to help Eileen and our situation. Despite my outburst during the surprise pregnancy episode in the late 1970s, there was never any question of me leaving my marriage, because I loved Eileen and the children too much and I would never break the promise I made on the altar when we were married.

Eileen saw the sun changing right before her eyes, but I saw a human being, Eileen, change right before my eyes. During the full ten years of the 1980s, when I was ignorant of her unfaithfulness, we stayed together, we worked together, had some good times and bad, happy times and sad, but during all this time I felt that Eileen's feelings for me lacked that real spontaneous, unconditional love that we used to have. It seemed to be easier to get her to promise to be faithful, than her love. I always had hope that the situation would change, but had no idea how, and the last avenue to such a complete change of heart and mind I would have expected her to walk down was a spiritual one. When God brought her back to him and she told me that all through the 1980s she had been unfaithful, I found it hard to come to terms with. Even though, through the mercy of God, I had felt this wonderful love and togetherness for the first time in fifteen years, I also felt a niggling hurt inside that persisted. On our first visit ever to Lourdes, Eileen and I went to the grotto at eleven o'clock one night and, kneeling there, I gave this hurt to Our Blessed Lady. A very emotional but most beautiful feeling came over me, and I knew there and then that I had finally, really forgiven, and the hurt disappeared permanently.

I feel now that what Eileen has done with her wonderful gift of faith will be of tremendous benefit to the future lives of our children. Through her courage in writing this book and her total commitment to doing the will of God, she has set a marvellous precedent for them — by admitting to faults, using mistakes as lessons, breaking down barriers that inhibit discussing family problems, inspiring confidence, openness and trust, and proving that any difficulty can be overcome, no matter how serious, by putting all your trust in Jesus Christ.

From a professional point of view, I have never seen or worked with a more dedicated, tirelessly efficient worker in all my years in the music business. She was never a 'clock watcher', I've never heard her complaining about being overworked, she gave all she had whether there were three or three thousand in our audience — she never really deserved to be unhappy.

At this moment I feel a little like director Joe Dowling did on the stairs that night in the Gaiety. After over thirty tumultuous years I can finally smile, put out my hand and say, 'I've never really met you until now — hello Eileen Reid!'